Classical Rhetoric
for
Contemporary Writing

By

Michelle Smith

Table of Contents

Introduction

Welcome, budding authors, to a unique training ground, where we will approach the art of writing with the precision and dedication of a professional athlete. I was once, like you, a student in an english composition class. I hated it. I was at college to play basketball, I thought, what did I possibly have to learn from a writing class? I was a young college athlete with eyes fixed solely on the hardwood of the basketball court. My days were consumed by drills, practice, games, and the relentless pursuit of athletic excellence. Yet in that first term, I found myself enrolled in a writing class, a requirement that seemed entirely unrelated to my life. Writing? What did that have to do with basketball? What did it have to do with me? Didn't I finish this stuff in high school?

I sat through those early classes with arms crossed, a frown etched across my face. Every assignment was a struggle, every critique a personal affront. The words on the page felt as foreign to me as speaking another language. It seemed ridiculous to spend time pondering over sentence structures when I could be perfecting my jump shot. What was the point? It didn't help that I was doing poorly in class...

Slowly, something started to change. As the weeks passed, I began to realize if I didn't change I wasn't going to make it through college. I decided to look at the situation differently. I decide to approach writing like I approached my game. In doing this I began to see similarities between the discipline of writing and the sport I loved so much. The more I wrote, the more I recognized the precision required to craft a sentence was akin to the precision of executing a play on the court. The versatility needed to shift between writing styles reminded me of playing different positions on the basketball floor.

Bit by bit I fell in love with writing.

The activities we did in class were no longer tedious drills but exciting challenges. I began to see that expanding my vocabulary was like adding new shots to my repertoire. Crafting a well-structured essay was like constructing a winning game strategy. Every word I penned, every sentence I built, became a reflection of my passion, not just for basketball but for expressing myself.

As the semesters rolled on, I realized something profound: my athletic training was not just shaping me as a basketball player; it was shaping me as a writer, a student, a thinker. The discipline, the commitment, the pursuit of excellence I learned on the court were transferable skills. They helped me through school, through life.

I once hated that writing class. I once thought it had nothing to do with my life as a basketball player. But as I grew to love writing, I understood that the game of words was as beautiful, as challenging, and as rewarding as the game of basketball.

Today, I play both games with equal passion. Whether on the court with my daughters or behind a desk, I'm playing to win. And every defeat, whether in a game or on a page, still contains a secret—the secret to the next victory. I'm forever grateful for that writing class that taught me to see the game in a whole new light. It's a lesson I carry with me, every word, every play, every day.

This textbook is the textbook I wish I had when I was in your seat. I am approaching the task of teaching writing as I would approach coaching an athlete. I'll often return to my favorite sport, basketball, but I will often try to extend the analogy to other sports. So imagine you are a player on the court. Just as basketball is a game of agility, teamwork, and technique, so too is writing a game of words, structure, and intent. This isn't just about putting words on a page; this is about crafting prose that lands exactly where you aim. In the words of my greatest writing teacher: "Good writing is writing that has exactly the effect the author intends." Let's dive into how this book, akin to a basketball training manual, will guide you to that goal.

1. The Playbook - Your Roadmap to Success:

This book is not merely a collection of words; it's a comprehensive guide, your training playbook. Like a coach who instructs his players to execute plays with perfection, this book will guide you through the various techniques and strategies required to make your writing have exactly the effect you intend.

2. Drills and Vocabulary - Building Your Offensive Game:

The first step to winning the game of writing is building your vocabulary, akin to a basketball player learning different shots. New words are your offensive arsenal. From three-pointers to slam dunks, different plays require different skills. Similarly, different contexts in writing require various words. This section of the book is a hands-on guide to expanding your vocabulary, helping you find the exact words to nail those crucial points.

3. Rhetorical Forms - Defensive Strategies:

A good defense in basketball is about structure, formation, and anticipation. Likewise, good writing is about knowing various rhetorical forms or structures to place your words. This book will teach you these structures, helping you construct sentences, paragraphs, and essays that flow smoothly, creating a coherent and effective defense against misunderstanding and ambiguity.

4. Reading Above Your Level - Playing with the Pros:

Just as aspiring basketball players learn by watching and playing against those slightly above their skill level, so too can writers. Reading works that challenge you is like playing against a better opponent; it forces you to stretch, adapt, and grow. This section of the book will guide you in selecting and analyzing texts that will push your boundaries, bringing you closer to the writing level you aim to reach.

5. Putting It All Together - The Championship Game:

This book culminates in practical activities and real-world examples that integrate vocabulary, rhetorical forms, and challenging reading materials. It's like the drills before the championship game, the practice that makes perfect, the repetition that leads to victory. Remember, "Good writing is writing that has exactly the effect the author intends." Every chapter, every exercise brings you closer to that winning shot in writing.

Playing to Win:

Good writing is no accident. It's a craft honed through diligent practice, careful strategy, and relentless pursuit of excellence. Like winning a basketball game, it requires knowing the right moves, executing them with precision, and constantly learning from those who are a step ahead. This book is your coach, your teammate, and your playbook. It's designed to help you learn new words, understand rhetorical structures, and engage with writing that challenges you.

Just as every defeat in basketball contains a secret—the secret to the next victory—every struggle in writing contains a lesson, a path to success. This book is about turning those lessons into victories, one word, one sentence, one essay at a time.

Are you ready to take the court and play the game of writing at a championship level? Then lace up your literary sneakers, grab this book, and let's begin the journey. Welcome to the big leagues.

Words

If we want to improve our game we need better skills. In writing there are two main skills. First is learning new words. Second is learning new rhetorical forms or structures (you can think of these as types of sentences) in which to put those new words. In this section we will be learning new words and learning them intimately.

English is more than a mere method of communication; it's a living, breathing entity that has evolved and adapted through the ages, much like a seasoned athlete refining their game. From its earliest origins to its current global dominance, English showcases a fascinating history that offers valuable insights for every writer. Let's explore this journey together, sprinkling in a few coaching insights and anticipating where the English language might be headed next.[1]

1. Proto-Indo-European Era (circa 4500-2500 BCE) - The Origins:

This foundational period is where it all began. Much like the basic training drills in sports, the Proto-Indo-European language laid the groundwork for what would become English. Words like "mother" and "father" have

---

[1] Much of this chapter owes a debt to research conducted in the Oxford English Dictionary and interested students should use their University Library to explore that rich resource for more.

roots in this ancient language, giving us a sense of connection across millennia.

Picture the foundations of a vast stadium, the initial blueprints for an expansive sporting complex, where every brick laid and every plan made leads to something monumental. Similarly, the Proto-Indo-European (PIE) era is the foundational groundwork of what would eventually grow into the English language, among others.

In a sense, the Proto-Indo-European language is the ancient locker room where linguistic strategies were first formulated. During this time, communities that spoke the same language were relatively close-knit, similar to a close team of athletes. Over time, as these communities spread across Europe and Asia, their languages evolved in different directions, leading to the formation of various linguistic branches.

Much like the basic training an athlete undergoes to build fundamental skills, understanding the PIE roots helps us comprehend the core structure and etymology of the words we use today. For example, the PIE root "méh₂tēr" gives us the word "mother," and the root "ph₂tér" leads to "father." These roots can be traced across different Indo-European languages, revealing a shared heritage.

The influence of Proto-Indo-European is not just confined to familial terms. Roots of many basic elements, concepts, and natural phenomena were also formed during this period. The sun, moon, water, and earth have corresponding PIE roots that have branched out into various languages.

Understanding this era is akin to understanding the fundamental rules and strategies of a sport. It provides a foundation, a starting point that reveals the underlying principles guiding the game. For writers and language enthusiasts, diving into the Proto-Indo-European era is an exploration of the very origins of communication, the birth of a method that has allowed humanity to convey thoughts, emotions, and ideas.

Just as an athlete must know the basic rules to play the game effectively, a writer who grasps the ancient roots of language can play with words with a depth of understanding, creating expressions that resonate across time. The Proto-Indo-European era is not merely history; it's the opening chapter in the playbook of English, setting the stage for a game that continues to unfold and evolve. It's the training ground from which all subsequent plays were made, a timeless coach whispering the secrets of the game through the ages.

2. Old English (circa 500-1150 AD) - Building the Foundations:

During this time, English began to take shape. Think of it as the formative years of a young athlete, developing skills and finding identity. Old English brought us epic works like "Beowulf," illustrating the rich literary potential of the language.

Imagine a basketball team's transition from a small local league to a more competitive, challenging environment. The skills have been laid down; the basics are in place. Now it's time to hone those skills, create new plays, and build on what's already there.

Old English is this next step in the evolution of the language, akin to this transitional phase for a team. During this period, Germanic tribes such as the Angles, Saxons, and Jutes invaded Britain, mingling their languages and forming what would be recognized as Old English. This was a period of fusion and formation, a blend of influences that, much like a team incorporating new strategies, began to develop a distinct identity.

During the Old English era, we see the language form into something more complex and structured. If Proto-Indo-European was the drawing up of the fundamental plays, then Old English was the practice, the daily grind, the sweat and effort that turns a basic skill into an art form. It's the time of Beowulf, an epic poem that stands as a monument to the beauty and power of the language during this period.

There were no silent letters, and the grammar was highly inflected, with a complex system of declensions, much like a nuanced playbook full of intricate plays and movements. Words like "strong" and "water" come from this era, concrete and fundamental, words that have stood the test of time, much like a well-executed basic play in basketball.

In Old English, words were forged with a clear purpose and meaning, a directness that mirrors the simplicity and effectiveness of a well-practiced layup or free throw. The creation of kingdoms in England during this time also mirrors the formation of leagues and competitive structures in sports, each with their own styles, dialects, and ways of playing the game.

The importance of the Old English period in understanding contemporary English can be likened to knowing the history and strategies of basketball legends. By studying the plays, techniques, and styles of the past, current players and fans can appreciate the game's beauty and complexity on a deeper level.

In the game of writing, this era provides us with a solid playing field, a court on which the language began to dribble, pass, and score. It's the time when English started playing the game in earnest, building on the foundations, perfecting the craft, and setting the stage for the exciting developments to come.

In summary, the Old English era is where the language began to find its rhythm, its flow, its style. It's where the English language started to play the game with confidence, developing strategies and tactics that continue to influence the way we communicate today. It's a pivotal chapter in the playbook of English, a period of growth and formation, much like a basketball team transitioning from basics to competitive play. It's where the game truly began.

3. Middle English (circa 1150-1500 AD) - Transition and Growth:

As in a pivotal season for a team, Middle English marked a time of transformation. The Normans' invasion introduced French words like "court" and "judge," diversifying the linguistic repertoire and adding new dimensions.

Picture a soccer team that has mastered the basics and has developed its own unique style. But now, the game is changing. New players are introduced, and the rules are shifting. This team must adapt, innovate, and grow to remain competitive. This challenging, transformative phase is analogous to the era of Middle English.

The Middle English period is marked by profound changes, much like a soccer team undergoing a series of reforms, bringing in international players, and adapting to new regulations. The Norman Conquest of 1066 had a substantial influence on the English language. French became the language of the court, law, and church, while English continued to be used by the common people. This blending of French and Old English led to the development of Middle English, a rich and complex evolution of the language.

Chaucer's "Canterbury Tales" is to Middle English what a classic match is to soccer. It's a showcase of skill, strategy, and artistry. The diverse characters in Chaucer's work reflect the various dialects and social classes of the time, akin to the different playing styles seen in various soccer clubs.

During this period, English spelling began to be standardized, though it was still more phonetic than it is today. The grammar started to simplify, losing many of the inflections seen in Old English. Just as a soccer team refines its strategies, cutting unnecessary moves and focusing on efficiency, Middle English started to become more streamlined and accessible.

The influence of Latin through the church and academia also played a significant role in shaping Middle English. It added a layer of complexity, elegance, and precision, like the introduction of more refined strategies and plays within the game of soccer.

Words like "government," "council," and "parliament" were introduced during this time, reflecting the growing complexity of society and governance. Similarly, as soccer became more organized and widespread, new strategies, roles, and positions were defined, reflecting a growing sophistication in how the game was played.

The transition from Old to Middle English is not merely a linguistic shift; it's a societal, cultural, and intellectual evolution. It's a period of growth and expansion, much like the development of soccer from a local pastime to a global phenomenon.

In sum, the era of Middle English is a significant phase in the development of the English language, analogous to a soccer team's transition from regional competition to playing on the international stage. It's a time of adaptation, innovation, and refinement, where the language embraced new influences and evolved into something more versatile, nuanced, and expressive. Just as a soccer team grows through new challenges, learning from its international counterparts, the English language during this time embraced a new complexity and breadth that continue to enrich our communication today. It's a period where English didn't just play the game; it changed the game.

4. Early Modern English (circa 1500-1700 AD) - A New Level of Sophistication:

This was the age of Shakespeare, a literary MVP who expanded English in ways never before seen. Words like "assassination" and "lonely" were coined during this period, as the language reached new heights of expressiveness.

Think of a tennis player who has gone through rigorous training, learning the techniques and strategies, and now enters a new era of competition, aiming for a higher level of performance. The game's complexity increases, the plays become more sophisticated, and every serve, every stroke is executed with precision. This elevated state of the game can be likened to the era of Early Modern English.

This period marked the Renaissance, a time of cultural rebirth and intellectual revitalization. In tennis, a player might reevaluate their game, adopting new techniques, improving their fitness, and striving for perfection. Similarly, English during this time was characterized by an intense interest in learning, exploration, and artistic expression.

William Shakespeare, the Roger Federer of the English language, played the linguistic court with unparalleled grace and creativity. His works demonstrate the richness and complexity of Early Modern English, offering a masterclass in linguistic agility and flair. Whether it was the poetic serve of a sonnet or the volleys of dialogue in a play, Shakespeare's language was a game of beauty, depth, and virtuosity.

The printing press played a role akin to the spread of televised tennis matches, standardizing the language and making it accessible to a wider audience. Books became more available, and literacy rates increased. Like watching top tennis players, reading the works of great writers inspired others to learn and emulate, lifting the overall level of play.

During this time, vocabulary expanded significantly with the introduction of Latin and Greek words, much like a tennis player expanding their repertoire of shots and strategies. Words like "critic," "method," and "logic" entered the language, reflecting a more scholarly and systematic approach to thinking.

The grammar further simplified during this period, shedding unnecessary complexities, much like a tennis player refining their game to focus on what truly matters. This shift made the language more adaptable and versatile, ready to serve different roles and audiences.

Just as the tennis court's dimensions remain the same whether you're a beginner or a professional, the fundamental structure of English remained consistent. But within that framework, the language reached new heights of sophistication, just as a professional tennis player operates at a higher level of skill, strategy, and finesse.

In conclusion, the era of Early Modern English is the time when the language stepped onto a global stage, ready to compete, to challenge, to inspire. It's a period marked by creativity, exploration, and refinement, where the rules were not changed but elevated to an art form. It's when English donned its tennis whites, picked up the racquet, and played with the grace and skill that continue to captivate us today. The echoes of this time still resonate in the way we speak and write, a testament to a game well played, a match that set the standards for the modern era.

5. Contemporary English (1700 AD to present) - Global Dominance:

Today's English is like a star athlete playing on an international stage. It has absorbed words from languages worldwide, like "piano" from Italian or "yoga" from Sanskrit. It's a rich and diverse language, capable of capturing the nuances of our globalized world.

This period marks a period of global dominance and unprecedented reach. During the 18th and 19th centuries, the Industrial Revolution fueled technological advancement and societal changes, while the British Empire spread the English language to various parts of the globe. The standardization of English led to a more consistent and accessible means of communication, much like a common tool understood by many.

As the 20th century unfolded, the World Wars further extended the reach of English, showcasing its adaptability and versatility. It became a language that transcended borders, connecting people from different cultures and backgrounds. The advent of television and the internet only accelerated this spread, as English media reached every corner of the world. The language was not merely a tool for communication but a cultural phenomenon that shaped how people thought, worked, and interacted.

In the 21st century, globalization has cemented English's position as the lingua franca of business, science, technology, and diplomacy. Its presence is ubiquitous, and its influence is inescapable. The digital era has further woven English into the fabric of everyday life, allowing instantaneous sharing and connection. The impact of artificial intelligence and learning language models has been transformative, shaping the way English is understood, taught, and used.

The future of English is promising yet uncertain. The language is continuously evolving, reflecting the intermingling of cultures and the rise of digital communication. New dialects and forms may emerge, and technology will undoubtedly play a vital role in defining how English is experienced and expressed.

Contemporary English's journey from local roots to global dominance mirrors the human experience in a rapidly changing world. Its ability to adapt, innovate, and embrace new influences has made it a living, thriving entity that resonates with people from all walks of life. The language's rich history and its trajectory towards the future speak to its resilience, relevance, and endless potential. It's a testament to our shared humanity, a bridge between cultures, and a path to understanding in a world that is increasingly interconnected.

The Future - A Game in Evolution:

As we look to the future, English shows no signs of slowing down. Globalization and technology are driving new changes. Artificial Intelligence and Learning Language Models are reshaping how we write and communicate, providing tools to enhance our understanding and mastery of the language.

Imagine a seasoned coach employing state-of-the-art technology to train and guide a team. That's where English is headed, embracing the digital age, integrating with technology, and expanding its reach and influence.

In the future, the impact of Artificial Intelligence may enable even more precise and personalized communication, just as advanced training techniques allow athletes to fine-tune their skills. Additionally, the globalization of English ensures its continued evolution, absorbing new words and ideas from cultures around the world.

Conclusion:

English is indeed a great language, rich in history, diverse in its influences, and dynamic in its evolution. From its humble beginnings to its global dominance, it's a language that continues to inspire and connect us.

The game of English is far from over. With technology's role, including the advancement of Artificial Intelligence and the continuous impact of globalization, who knows where English will take us next? As writers, learners, and communicators, we're part of this exciting journey, playing on a field that's ever-expanding and full of potential. Let's

embrace the game, for in every defeat contains a secret—
the secret to the next victory.

With that, here are some words that are probably just
beyond your current vocabulary and a bit about them.

Definition of Ameliorate:

Improvement or Enhancement:

"Ameliorate" is a verb that signifies the act of making something
better, especially something that is unsatisfactory or
problematic. Whether applied to social, political, or economic
issues, or personal circumstances, the term embodies the
process of improvement or enhancement. It's about taking
steps to alleviate difficulties or defects, transforming
something challenging into something more favorable and
tolerable.

Etymology of Ameliorate:

Latin Roots:

The term "ameliorate" originates from the Latin word "melior,"
which translates to "better." This Latin root forms the basis of
the word, carrying a consistent theme of improvement.

Late Latin and Old French Influence:

The word evolved into "ameliorare" in Late Latin, meaning "to make better," and then made its way into Old French as "améliorer," with a similar connotation. This Romance language transition helped shape the word into its modern form.

Adoption into English:

During the 18th century, "ameliorate" was adopted into the English language, maintaining the sense of improving or making something better. The specific form and meaning in English can also be attributed to the influence of certain French verbs, signifying the continuity of the concept across languages.

The definition and etymology of "ameliorate" highlight a word steeped in a desire for positive change and growth. It's a term that resonates with the human endeavor to improve conditions, find solutions, and strive for a better state of affairs. The linguistic journey of "ameliorate" from Latin to English encapsulates a timeless and universal aspiration to enhance and elevate.

Examples:

1767 - Sow oats after a fallow or some ameliorating crop. (at ameliorating adj.)—A. Young
1779 - The probability of their lot being so much ameliorated.—H. Swinburne
1789–96 - The state of things is rapidly ameliorating.—J. Morse

1813 - A sterile soil..may be ameliorated by the application of quick lime.—H. Davy

1849 - In every human being there is a wish to ameliorate his own condition.—T. B. Macaulay

1879 - Gardeners and breeders..ameliorate..the plants and animals in which they are interested.—tr. A. de Quatrefages de Bréau

1882 - [Man]..would find his way back as the climate ameliorated.—Geikie in Macmillan's Mag.

Definitions of Lord:

Nobility Title:

> In a feudal or monarchical context, "Lord" refers to a title of nobility or honor. It is used to address a man who holds a particular position of authority, such as a baron or earl, or who owns a large estate. The title is a mark of respect and denotes a certain social status. It can be inherited or granted, and it often carries specific responsibilities and privileges within the realm.

God or Deity:

> In religious contexts, "Lord" is often used as a reference to God or a deity. Many religious traditions utilize this term to signify reverence, worship, and submission to the divine. In Christianity, for example, "Lord" is used to address Jesus Christ, reflecting acknowledgment of his divine nature and supreme authority.

Master or Ruler:

> The word "Lord" can also be used more broadly to signify someone who has authority, control, or power over others. This could be a ruler, master, or employer who exercises control over subjects, servants, or employees. It has also historically been used by wives when talking to their husbands. Sometimes this usage is preserved but acquires an ironic tone. The term used as "master" emphasizes dominance,

guidance, or protectorship, and it may be used metaphorically or literally to describe relationships in various contexts.

Courtesy Title:

In the United Kingdom, "Lord" can be a courtesy title for the younger sons of a duke or marquess. It's a form of address that is part of traditional aristocratic nomenclature and distinguishes certain individuals within the nobility. While it carries a certain prestige, it may not always be associated with substantive power or authority.

Legal or Official Usage:

In legal and governmental contexts, "Lord" may be part of a title for certain high-ranking officials. For example, in the United Kingdom, judges of the Supreme Court are referred to as "Lords Justices," and members of the House of Lords bear this title as well. Here, the term conveys a sense of authority and respect within the specific function of law and governance.

The etymology of the word "Lord" traces back to Old English and Germanic roots. Here's a look at its linguistic evolution:

Old English: The term originated from the Old English word "hlāford," which was a compound of "hlāf" (loaf) and "weard" (keeper or guardian). In this context, "hlāford" literally meant "loaf-ward" or "bread-keeper" and symbolized the one who provided sustenance or protection to others, such as a head of a household or a leader.

Middle English: During the Middle English period, the term evolved into "laverd" or "lord." The meaning began to broaden, encompassing not only heads of households but also rulers and noblemen.

Old High German: The Germanic influence on the term can be seen in the Old High German word "hlafward," with similar components and meanings to the Old English version.

Proto-Germanic Roots: Going even further back, the word can be traced to Proto-Germanic roots, with "*hlāibaz" meaning "loaf" and "*wardaz" meaning "keeper" or "guardian."

The progression of the word "Lord" from its earliest roots to its modern usage reflects a shift from a practical and specific role (a provider of bread) to a more symbolic and expansive concept (a person of authority, nobility, or divinity). The etymology of "Lord" paints a picture of societal development and changing perceptions of leadership and responsibility. It's a fascinating linguistic journey that connects everyday life to broader themes of power and reverence.

Examples are too numerous to cite.

Definition of Neck:

Anatomical Structure:

The neck is the part of the body that connects the head to the torso. It includes muscles, ligaments, and bones like the cervical vertebrae, supporting the head and housing vital structures such as the trachea and esophagus.

To Strike on the Neck, to Stun, Kill, or Behead:

The term "neck" can be used as a verb to describe the act of striking on the neck with the intent to stun, kill, or behead. This action may be associated with certain historical or cultural practices, including forms of capital punishment or hunting techniques.

To Drink or Eat Greedily:

"Necking" can also refer to the act of drinking or eating greedily. Whether downing a beverage in one go or consuming food with excessive enthusiasm, this colloquial expression captures a sense of indulgence and haste.

To Fondle or Kiss:

In a more intimate context, "necking" describes the act of fondling or kissing, especially in a romantic or affectionate manner. It's a term that conveys physical closeness and emotional connection, often associated with courtship or passion.

To Tie Down or Secure:

The verb "to neck" may also signify the act of tying down, fastening, or securing something. It could refer to binding objects tightly at a particular point, resembling the narrow connection that characterizes a neck. This usage extends to various practical applications, from securing loads during transport to tying down equipment.

Narrow Connecting Part:

Finally, "neck" can denote the narrow, elongated part connecting two wider parts of an object or structure. This definition can apply to various contexts, like the neck of a bottle or the neck of a guitar, referring to slender portions that bridge larger segments.

The word "neck" encapsulates a broad spectrum of meanings, spanning anatomical, violent, indulgent, romantic, practical, and structural aspects. Its versatile applications reflect the complex and rich tapestry of the English language, linking different facets of human life and experience through a single term.

The term "neck" has an intriguing etymology that traces its roots to multiple languages and historical periods. The English word "neck" comes from the Old English "hnecca," which meant the neck of a person or the long, slender part of a thing. It's further connected to the Proto-Germanic word "hnakkaz," which has cognates in Old Norse "hnakki," Old Frisian "hnek," Old High German "hnac," and German "Nacken," all referring to the neck.

These Germanic origins might be traced back to the Proto-Indo-European root "*knok-", a term of obscure origin, but likely linked to the notion of high or upward, possibly pointing to the neck's position as the upward extension of the body. The word's evolution and connections across different languages underscore its foundational significance in describing a fundamental part of human and animal anatomy, as well as its metaphorical extensions to various objects and actions.

Examples. Try to guess which usage is which:

1518 - She couthe well..necke a mesure, her smyrkynge gan her sale She made ten shylynge, of one barell of ale.

1653 - As if the Protestant Religion were neckt in the sparring blowes.

1712 - Like thy bold Sires in Forty-Eight, Who neck'd their Prince, a worthy Fate!

1729 - Caligula who rather Wisht all the folk of Rome had but one neck That he might neck them all at once together.

1825 - Let's see nae mair o' Peter Wallett's neckin' an' touslin' here. (at necking n.1 2).

1842 - Newcastle... I came rather suddenly upon a man who unceremoniously put his arm round a young lady, and..said..'I was only a-necking on her a little bit, Sir.'

1857 - The usual practice of farmers whenever they want work oxen, is to..neck together, with ropes, as many pair of..steers as they desire.—D. E. E. Braman

1860 - Neck, to swallow.—J. C. Hotten

1877 - When sufficiently near him, she necked her supposed partner, greeting him with the following affectionate salute.—G. Fraser

1882 - Neck, to kill fowls by pulling their necks out, or rabbits by giving them a blow on the back of the neck.—G. F. Jackson

1889 - He neck'd a good share o' beer that neet o' th' jewbilee.—E. Peacock

1899 - He wasn't selling 'is meat over-quick, 'cos 'alf the time he was necking four-ale in the pub 'cross the way.—C. Rook

1924 - Some of those janes certainly could neck, and they were ready for it any time.—P. Marks

1932 - I say! He's necked the whole box of chocolates, and left none for his sister.—A. J. Worrall

1933 - Necking, in range terminology... On the range an unruly cow or one with roving proclivities will often be necked or tied to a more tractable animal.—J. V. Allen

1935 - Do you know who that is that this necker is necking?.. My girl. No less.—P. G. Wodehouse

1950 - That this rapscallion was necking with his legal bride.—G. Barker

1970 - The best behaved teenager necks.—G. Greer

1995 - I worked out that Prozac and alcohol tend to mix really well— so I necked another Prozac, downed a couple more pints.—DJ

1999 - Toyah is being necked by a hunk.—Sunday Sport

2000 - She could easily save a hundred quid in a week just by not being at home necking endless vodka cranberries.—V. Routledge

2002 - By the time I caught up with the three of them the poor old Hare was gasping his last, so..I reached in and necked him.

Definition of Polymath:

Individual with Profound Knowledge in Various Subjects:

A polymath is a person who possesses extensive knowledge and expertise in several different subjects or fields of study. Unlike a specialist, who focuses on one particular area, a polymath's understanding spans a wide range of disciplines. This depth and breadth of knowledge enable the individual to make connections and synthesize information across various domains.

Renaissance Person:

The term "polymath" is often associated with the ideal of the Renaissance person, epitomized by historical figures like Leonardo da Vinci. In this context, a polymath is not only knowledgeable in various academic fields such as mathematics, science, literature, and the arts, but also skilled in practical areas like music, painting, or physical pursuits. The Renaissance person embodies a harmonious blend of intellectual curiosity, artistic creativity, and physical capability.

Modern Multidisciplinary Expert:

In contemporary times, a polymath may refer to an individual who excels in multiple professional or technical fields. This modern interpretation emphasizes not just theoretical understanding but also the practical application of knowledge across disciplines. Whether in business, technology, or the arts, a modern polymath leverages a diverse skill set to innovate and problem-solve.

The term "polymath" has its roots in the Greek words "πολύς" (polus), meaning "many," and "μανθάνω" (manthanein), meaning "to learn." Together, they form the word "πολυμαθής" (polymathēs), which translates to "having learned much."

Introduced into English in the early 17th century, "polymath" has maintained the original Greek meaning, encapsulating the idea of an individual who has acquired extensive and profound knowledge across various subjects or disciplines.

This etymology, with its connection to the original Greek lettering, provides a rich insight into the term's essence. It not only defines the polymath as someone with diverse intellectual pursuits but also connects the modern reader to a classical ideal that has been celebrated and aspired to for centuries. The term "polymath" stands as a testament to human curiosity, intellectual versatility, and the timeless value of comprehensive learning.

Examples:

1624 - To be thought and held Polumathes and Polihistors.—R. Burton
1806 - The Polymaths and Polyhistors, Polyglotts and all their sisters.—T. Moore
1897 - One of the last of the mighty Scots polymaths.—O. Smeaton

1919 - The masters of the subtle schools are controversial, polymath.—T. S. Eliot

1987 - Scott was..noted as something of a polymath, being interested in literature, languages, science and theology.— W. Raeper

1997 - Alberti was but the first in a rapid succession of brilliant polymath Renaissance scholars.—J. Satinover

Definition of Proforma:

Preliminary or Provisional Document:

In a business context, a proforma invoice or statement is a
preliminary document that provides an estimate of what the
final invoice will look like. It's often used in international trade
to provide details about the goods being shipped, their value,
weight, and other relevant information. This document is not
legally binding and does not serve as a demand for payment
but is more of an informational tool to facilitate the
transaction.

Financial Statement or Projection:

Proforma can also refer to financial statements that are prepared
in advance of a planned transaction, such as a merger or
acquisition. These statements present the expected financial
impact of the transaction, using certain assumptions and
projections. They are utilized to model how changes in
different variables might affect the company's financial
position in the future. It's a valuable tool for decision-making
and strategic planning.

For the Sake of Form or as a Formal Gesture:

The term "proforma" can also mean something done for the sake
of form or as a matter of protocol. It can refer to actions or
procedures carried out to comply with conventional rules or
etiquette but lacking genuine substance or significance. For
example, a proforma resignation might be submitted to fulfill

a formal requirement, even if the decision has already been made.

The term "proforma" comes from the Latin phrase "pro forma," which translates to "for the sake of form" or "as a matter of form."

The Latin word "pro" means "for" or "on behalf of," and "forma" means "form" or "shape." Together, they convey the idea of something done in a customary or prescribed manner, following a specific form or protocol.

In the business and legal contexts, this term has been adopted to refer to documents or actions that are done according to a particular format or for the sake of fulfilling a formality. Over time, it has evolved to encompass various meanings, including those related to provisional invoices and financial statements, reflecting the importance of formal procedures and documentation in these fields.

The adoption of this Latin phrase into English legal and commercial terminology highlights the influence of classical language on modern professional jargon, maintaining a connection to the traditional concepts of form and process.

Examples:

1572 - The learned Papiste..commeth [to Holy Communion] onely for feare of punishement, or pro forma tantum, for fashion sake.—J. Whitgift
1623 - Which is thought to be done rather pro formâ than ex animo.—J. Chamberlain

1712 - The Prime Vizir told the Plenipotentiaries, only pro formâ, that we should be Keffils of their Promises contained in the forementioned Attestation.—R. Sutton

1823 - I soon saw, that it was only a pro forma dinner, and that there was nothing of cordiality in all the civility with which we were treated.—J. Galt

1836 - An Appendix containing pro-forma invoices, Account Sales, Bills of Lading and Bills of Exchange.—Times

1836 - Actual and pro forma statements of British and foreign invoices and account sales.—Times

1849 - The doctrines of Buddha are pro formâ professed by a very few.—Jrnl. Royal Geogr. Soc.

1867 - His speech in the House is simply a pro forma rehearsal of propositions with which everybody is familiar.—N. Amer. Rev.

1928 - He rejoiced in inventing new Army Forms, which he called 'pro forma's'... Some of them were such that one's best information could not find a heading in them.—E. Blunden

1959 - It became a matter of extreme difficulty to make the usual conservative forecast of the final selling price, or pro forma valuation as it was called.—A. Gaitskell

1988 - Hawes thanked him pro forma on 31 March.—B. Cooper

1999 - Importation follow-up and EC documents must be filed..and a 'pro-forma' bill prepared prior to shipping.—J. G. Cruickshank

2000 - Application[s] on prescribed proforma are invited for pre-qualification from reputed..dry cleaners/launderers.—News (Karachi)

2003 - Unlike net income.., pro forma earnings are calculated in any number of ways.—D. L. Scott

2004 - A reporter would make a proforma visit to a remote location so that the already written story could bear a dateline.—New Yorker

Definition of Roustabout:

Oil Rig Worker:

In the context of the oil industry, a roustabout refers to an unskilled or semi-skilled laborer who performs general maintenance, manual labor, and basic tasks on an oil rig. This role often involves physically demanding work, such as lifting heavy objects, cleaning equipment, and assisting skilled workers like drillers and electricians.

Circus or Carnival Worker:

Within the world of circuses and carnivals, a roustabout is a laborer responsible for setting up, tearing down, and maintaining the equipment and grounds. They perform essential but often overlooked tasks that keep the circus or carnival running smoothly, ensuring that everything is in place for performers and attendees.

General Laborer or Unskilled Worker:

The term "roustabout" can also apply more broadly to an unskilled laborer who performs various manual tasks. In this general sense, it captures the notion of a jack-of-all-trades who might work in construction, shipping, or other industries that require physical effort and flexibility. The work might involve handling freight, building structures, or carrying out other labor-intensive tasks.

Disreputable or Vagabond Person:

Colloquially, "roustabout" may also describe a person with a disreputable or vagabond lifestyle. It could refer to someone who leads a transient existence, moving from place to place without a fixed home or occupation. This usage conveys a sense of restlessness or nonconformity, often associated with a disregard for social norms or conventional lifestyles.

The etymology of "roustabout" is a bit unclear, and the word's origins are somewhat elusive.

It is believed to have first appeared in American English in the mid-19th century. The term might be related to the English word "roust," which means to rouse or stir up, and could be linked to the roustabout's role in handling various demanding physical tasks.

Some have also suggested that it might be connected to the word "rouse," especially in the nautical sense, where "rouse" means to pull or haul strongly and briskly. Given that roustabouts were often involved in heavy lifting and manual labor, this connection is plausible.

Another possibility is that it's related to the British dialectical term "roust," meaning a strong current or rush of water, perhaps metaphorically likening the energy and force of a roustabout's work to a powerful flow of water.

The term has also been associated with rough or boisterous behavior, and this connotation might have contributed to the word's evolution, particularly in the sense of a disreputable or vagabond person.

In any case, the precise origins of "roustabout" remain somewhat mysterious, reflecting a word that has been shaped and reshaped by various industries and cultural contexts throughout its history.

Examples:

1860 - Every steamer has also a set of deck hands, 'roustabouts'—whose..duty it is..to load and unload freight. —Daily Cleveland (Ohio) Herald

1862 - We saw a large and excited crowd chasing a poor German who had the temerity and honesty to hurrah for Lincoln, when he was set upon by a lot of rowdies and roustabouts.—Philadelphia Inquirer

1871 - It would be difficult to imagine the erudite and abstruse Sumner..'going in' with the recklessness of a city rough or pot-house roustabout.—Fort Wayne (Indiana) Daily Sentinel

1872 - The Western rough is frequently a roustabout.—M. Schele de Vere

1875 - The performers all went to the Priest house, while the roustabouts immediately commenced to haul the poles, canvass, etc.—Decatur (Illinois) Daily Republican

1883 - Do you mean the Roman army?—those six sandalled roustabouts in nightshirts?—'M. Twain'

1886 - Teamsters and roustabouts were so hostile to this innovation [sc. an oil pipeline], which they regarded as an invasion of their rights, that the line had to be constantly guarded.—Harper's Mag.

1942 - I hear he is to have a big lump of money for this work he is doing like a roustabout on the docks in New Orleans.—E. Ferber

1960 - I've got a good wife, only we're temperamentally unsuited to one another. I'm too common for her. Too much of a roustabout.—H. Miller

1976 - From a carnival roustabout to owner of the show in 25 years.—Telegraph-Jrnl. (St. John, New Brunswick)

1996 - The workers charged with the erection of the circus tents are the roustabouts.—R. J. Reising

2007 - Members of the deck crews who worked as roustabouts carried cargo on and off the steamboat at river ports.—G. S. Pablis

2009 - You will need to be 18 or over for most offshore jobs... You could..join the industry as a roustabout or roughneck and work your way up.—Manch. Evening News

Definition of Sang-froid:

The term "sang-froid" is relatively specific in its meaning, and it doesn't typically have various distinct meanings. However, it can be applied and interpreted in different contexts. Here's a breakdown:

Composure Under Pressure:

Sang-froid is a French term that translates to "cold blood" in English. It refers to the ability to maintain calmness and composure in a stressful or challenging situation. People with sang-froid can think clearly, act deliberately, and maintain self-control even when under intense pressure or facing potential danger.

Emotional Detachment:

In some contexts, sang-froid might be associated with a certain level of emotional detachment or unflappability. It's not merely about staying calm under pressure but reflects a person's capacity to remain unaffected or unperturbed by emotional provocations. This aspect of sang-froid can be seen as a virtue in certain professions or scenarios, but it may also be perceived as a lack of empathy or warmth in interpersonal relations.

Historical and Cultural Connotations:

Sang-froid carries historical and cultural nuances, particularly in French history, where it has been associated with a certain stoicism and aristocratic demeanor. The ability to maintain one's poise, dignity, and rationality, regardless of external circumstances, has been admired and often idealized in various literary and historical contexts.

The etymology of "sang-froid" traces back to French origins, where the term is a compound of two words: "sang," meaning "blood," and "froid," meaning "cold." Together, they literally translate to "cold blood."

The expression reflects the idea of having blood that remains cool and unheated, even in situations that might cause others to become hot-blooded or impassioned. The metaphorical connection between temperature and emotional state is common in many languages, and in this case, it illustrates the quality of calmness and self-control, even when facing adversity or stress.

The term has been used in English since the 18th century, maintaining its original French spelling and pronunciation. It represents a cultural ideal of grace under pressure, emotional restraint, and rationality, and its etymology captures these qualities in a vivid and metaphorical way.

Examples:

1750 - Don Louis, with the same sang froid as constantly persisted, till he at last prevailed.—Ld. Chesterfield.
1790 - Sang~froid of a chess-player.—J. P. Andrews.
1823 - With great sang-froid.., he sat smoking Tobacco.—Byron.
1888 - Cameron..accepted the situation with his usual sang froid.—A. K. Green.

Definition of Schadenfreude:

Pleasure at Another's Misfortune:

> Schadenfreude is a German word that translates to "harm-joy" in English. It refers to the feeling of pleasure or satisfaction derived from someone else's misfortune, failure, or suffering. It is a complex and often controversial emotion, as it involves deriving joy from another person's distress.

Social and Psychological Contexts:

> In psychological and social contexts, Schadenfreude can be studied as a phenomenon related to envy, rivalry, or resentment. It may be experienced more intensely when the person suffering misfortune is perceived as arrogant, undeserving, or a rival. It is also related to the perception of justice or karma, where the misfortune is seen as a deserved comeuppance.

Cultural Perspectives:

> Different cultures might perceive and evaluate Schadenfreude in various ways. While it is often considered a negative or taboo emotion in many societies, some literary, philosophical, and cultural traditions explore it as a natural human response, reflecting deeper social dynamics and individual psychology.

The etymology of "Schadenfreude" comes directly from the German language, where it's a compound of two words: "Schaden," meaning "harm" or "damage," and "Freude," meaning "joy" or "pleasure."

This compound word succinctly captures the essence of the emotion: finding joy or pleasure in someone else's misfortune or suffering. It doesn't have a direct equivalent in English, which has led to the adoption of the German term into the English language.

The word first appeared in German texts in the 18th century and made its way into English usage in the 19th century. Its etymology reveals not only the literal meaning of the word but also the complexity and ambivalence of the emotion it describes. The juxtaposition of "harm" and "joy" in a single term provides a striking insight into an aspect of human psychology that can be both fascinating and unsettling.

Examples:

1852 - What a fearful thing is it that any language should have a word expressive of the pleasure which men feel at the calamities of others; for the existence of the word bears testimony to the existence of the thing. And yet in more than one such a word is found... In the Greek ἐπιχαιρεκακία, in the German, Schadenfreude.—R. C. Trench.

1901 - Sometimes it [sc. Queen Victoria's smile] would be coyly negative, leading the speaker on, the lips slightly opened, with a suggestion of kindly fun, even of a little innocent Schadenfreude. —Q. Rev.

1902 - I am persuaded that what (no doubt by a slip of undesigned candour) is described in the recent Life of Claude Bernard by an eminent English physiologist as the 'Joys of the Laboratory', are very real 'joys' to the vivisector; that is, Schadenfreude,—Pleasure in the Pain he witnesses and creates.—Contemp. Rev.

1920 - The particular sentiment described in German as schadenfreude 'pleasure over another's troubles' (how characteristic it is that there should be no equivalent in any other language for this peculiarly Teutonic emotion!) makes but little appeal to the average Briton except where questions of age and of failing powers come into play.—F. Hamilton.

1947 - The Schadenfreude of cooks at keyholes.—W. H. Auden.

1977 - Solidarity or no solidarity, Widger was not wholly without Schadenfreude at seeing his informative colleague discomfited for once.—'E. Crispin'.

Definition of Sesquipedalian:

The term "sesquipedalian" primarily carries two related meanings, each of which I've detailed below:

Pertaining to Long Words:

The word "sesquipedalian" can describe a word that is unusually long and characterized by multiple syllables. It's often used to refer to words that might be considered ostentatious or overly complex. In this sense, a sesquipedalian word is one that is lengthy and may be challenging to understand or pronounce.

A Style of Writing or Speaking:

"Sesquipedalian" can also describe a style of writing or speaking that is characterized by the use of long words and complex vocabulary. This usage might be employed for effect, to demonstrate erudition or intellectual prowess, or it might be criticized as pretentious and unnecessarily complicated. A person who utilizes sesquipedalian language may be attempting to impress an audience but risks alienating those who find the language overly ornate or inaccessible.

These two definitions are intertwined, with the term itself serving as a somewhat playful commentary on language that can be seen as excessively grand or elaborate. It reflects a tension between the desire for precision and eloquence and the risk of obscurity or pretension. he etymology of "sesquipedalian" comes from the Latin word "sesquipedalis," which literally translates to "a foot and a half long." The term is a combination of "sesqui-" meaning "one and a half" and "pes" (genitive "pedis") meaning "foot."

The word gained a metaphorical sense in reference to words and expressions that seemed overly long and cumbersome. The Roman poet Horace famously used the term in his work "Ars Poetica" (The Art of Poetry), where he criticized the use of unnecessarily long words, referring to them as "sesquipedalia verba," or "words a foot and a half long."

In English, "sesquipedalian" has maintained this metaphorical sense, describing words that are perceived as long, or a style of writing or speaking characterized by such words. The etymology of the term provides a colorful illustration of its meaning, likening long words to physical length and playfully commenting on the potential excesses of language.

Examples:
1656 - Sesquipedalian words (verba sesquipedalia) used by Horace for great, stout, and lofty words; words that are very long, consisting of many Syllables.—T. Blount.
1807 - The verses of Stephen Hawes are as full of barbarous sesquipedalian Latinisms, as the prose of the Rambler.—R. Southey.
1853 - Towards the end of her letter Miss Jenkyns used to become quite sesquipedalian.—E. C. Gaskell.
1861 - In these sesquipedalian compounds the significative root remains distinct.—F. Max Müller.

Definition of Sozzled:

"Sozzled" is a term primarily used informally, and its meaning is as follows:

Intoxicated or Drunk:

"Sozzled" is a slang term that describes the state of being intoxicated or drunk, typically due to the consumption of alcohol. It often conveys a sense of being not just mildly tipsy but rather heavily inebriated. The word might be used humorously or colloquially to describe someone who has had a bit too much to drink and is displaying the signs of intoxication, such as slurred speech, unsteady gait, or impaired judgment.

The word "sozzled" captures a specific aspect of intoxication, often reflecting a more lighthearted or humorous take on the condition. It's a term more likely to be found in casual conversation or humorous writing rather than in formal or serious contexts.

The etymology of "sozzled" is somewhat unclear, but it appears to be a slang term that originated in British English in the early 20th century.

Some sources suggest that "sozzled" may be linked to the word "soused," which has been used since the 17th century to mean "drunk" or "intoxicated," possibly stemming from the process of soaking or immersing something in liquid, particularly in alcohol.

Another theory points to a connection with "sozzle," a dialect word meaning to splash or spill, referring to the act of sloppily pouring a liquid, such as an alcoholic beverage.

Despite the lack of definitive origin, the term "sozzled" has been widely used to describe the state of being drunk, with its playful sound perhaps adding to its appeal in casual or humorous contexts. It continues to be a part of contemporary English slang, especially in the United Kingdom.

Examples:
1886-96 - She was thick in the clear, Fairly sosselled on beer.
    — in Farmer & Henley Slang.
1904 - It was customary to mix Tea, Egg~nog, and Straight
    Goods until the last Caller was Sozzled. — G. Ade.
1921 - I wasn't what you'd call sozzled. I might have been lit up
    a bit, but sozzled—no. — Blackwood's Mag.
1935 - He was beautifully sozzled last night. — D. L. Sayers.
1951 - 'Gin, blast it! T'hell with gin!' The voice gave a sozzled
    chuckle. — 'J. Wyndham'.
1963 - 'She'm sozzled,' said Wally, and indeed, it was so. — N.
    Marsh.
1972 - With a sozzled smile he began to sing about a little
    yellow dory. — E. Staebler.

Definition of Toothsome:

Delicious or Tasty:

"Toothsome" is often used to describe food that is delicious, appetizing, or pleasing to the taste. The term may be applied to a dish or specific food item that is considered particularly delectable.

Pleasing to the Eye; Attractive:

"Toothsome" can also describe something or someone that is attractive or pleasing to the eye. This sense of the word might be applied to a person who is considered good-looking or to an object or scene that is aesthetically pleasing.

Biting or Sharp:

The term "toothsome" may also refer to something that is biting or sharp, resembling a tooth in its ability to cut or pierce. This meaning can be applied to describe a physical object with a sharp edge, such as a tool or a blade, or metaphorically to describe speech or writing that has a biting or incisive quality.

These definitions encompass the sensory appeal of "toothsome," whether it's the pleasure of taste, the attraction of sight, or the cutting quality of something sharp and incisive. The term's range of meanings adds to its versatility in describing experiences or objects that engage the senses or the intellect in distinctive ways.

The etymology of "toothsome" is relatively straightforward and directly related to the English word "tooth."

Tooth: This part of the word refers to the hard, calcified structure found in the jaws of many vertebrates, used for biting and chewing.

-some: A suffix used in English to form adjectives, meaning "tending to" or "characterized by." In this context, it refers to something that is related to or has the quality of a tooth.

The word "toothsome" originated in the early 16th century, with the first recorded use in English appearing around 1530. The combination of "tooth" with the "-some" suffix leads to a literal interpretation of "toothsome" as "related to or having the quality of a tooth."

The development of "toothsome" to mean "tasty" or "delicious" seems to have arisen from the notion of something that is pleasant to bite or chew. The further extension of the term to mean "attractive" or "pleasing to the eye" likely came later, broadening the word's sensory appeal.

The meaning related to "biting" or "sharp" maintains the more literal connection to a tooth's cutting or piercing quality, tying back to the word's root in a more direct way.

The etymology of "toothsome" thus offers a window into the word's multifaceted meanings, reflecting a blend of the physical, sensory, and aesthetic.

Examples:

1551 - Speaking thinges nothing tothsome. — T. Wilson.

1565 - We found water, which although it were neither so toothsome as running water, yet did we not refuse it. — J. Sparke.

1601 - Whose malice (being as toothsome as the Adders sting). — T. Morley.

1604 - The Patattoes, which they eate as a delicate and toothsome meate. — E. Grimeston.

1805 - Elegant and toothsome sermons were most in request. — J. Ramsay.

1848 - The Earl is a toothsome man. — E. Bulwer-Lytton.

1899 - Hard to please if they cannot select something toothsome from the menu. — E. Callow.

Definition of Wassail:

A Celebratory Drink:

Wassail can refer to a hot mulled cider, flavored with spices and honey. It's a traditional drink consumed on the Twelfth Night of Christmas and other festive occasions. This beverage may include various blends of spices, wine, or ale, symbolizing celebration and goodwill.

A Toast:

As a toast, "wassail" can be used to wish good health to others. This expression is often raised in a glass, perhaps ironically during a mundane or non-celebratory moment, adding a touch of humor or sarcasm to an otherwise ordinary event. Someone might raise a glass of plain water and proclaim "Wassail!" to their friends on a Tuesday lunchtime, for example.

A Salutation:

The word "wassail" can also serve as a salutation, expressing goodwill. In a more ironic sense, it might be used in a casual greeting between friends or acquaintances, offering a humorous and unexpected twist to a regular "hello."

A Ritual or Ceremony:

Wassailing refers to a ritualistic practice conducted on the Twelfth Night of Christmas. This medieval English tradition involved singing and drinking to the health of apple trees to promote a good harvest. Participants, often called wassailers, would sing, make loud noises, and pour wassail on the tree roots.

A Type of Punch Bowl:

The term "wassail" may also refer to the container or punch bowl in which the wassail drink is served. Often ornate and decorative, these wassail bowls could be the centerpiece of the Twelfth Night celebrations.

A Festive Song or Carol:

Wassail songs, also known as wassailing songs, are traditional carols sung during the wassailing ceremony on the Twelfth Night of Christmas. Different regions have various wassail songs, expressing good wishes and prosperity.

A Person Participating in the Ritual:

During the wassail ritual, the person drinking from the wassail-bowl may specifically be referred to as the wassailer. This individual might play a special role in the celebration, leading others in song or toasting to the health of the trees.

"Wassail" is a multifaceted term that embraces a rich tradition blending culinary, social, and spiritual aspects. It resonates with warmth, community joy, and the continuity of ancient customs. Whether referencing the drink, the toast, the salutation, the ritual, the container, the song, or the participant, "wassail" connects us with a vivid and enduring cultural heritage.

Origins in Old Norse and Old English:

The term "wassail" has its origins in the Old Norse phrase "ves heill" (later "ver heill") and the Old English "wes hál," both meaning "be in good health" or "be fortunate." These expressions served as salutations, equivalent to "hail" or "farewell," in both Old English and Old Norse.

Transition to Drinking Formula:

Interestingly, there's no evidence in Old English, Old Norse, or other Germanic languages of these phrases being used as drinking formulas. The usage likely arose among the Danish-speaking inhabitants of England and eventually spread to the native population. By the 12th century, the Normans regarded it as characteristic of the English.

First Recorded Instances:

The earliest known occurrence is in Geoffrey of Monmouth's writings (circa 1140), where "wes heil" and "drinc heil" are found. However, this attribution to the 5th century is an anachronism. Various manuscripts of Wace's "Brut" (circa 1180) also contain forms of the word, as does his "Roman de Rou."

Drinking Complement - Drinkhail:

Alongside "wassail," the term "drinkhail" also emerged, with "heill" from Old Norse serving as a complement in both. The exact form of "drinkhail" is debatable, with influences from Old English or archaic Scandinavian, and it might parallel Old Norse's "sit heill," meaning "sit in health."

Cultural Significance and Development:

The transition of "wassail" from a greeting to a toast, a spiced beverage, a punch bowl, and a Twelfth Night ritual highlights the complexity and cultural richness of the term. The story of Rowena, the revelry before the Battle of Hastings, and the English students' celebration in Paris with "wessail" and "dringail" further weave the word into the historical and literary fabric of England.

Influence of Scandinavian and Germanic Roots:

The term's evolution, from its Old Norse and Old English beginnings to a multifaceted cultural symbol, reflects the mingling of Scandinavian and Germanic influences with native English traditions.

The word "wassail" is a fascinating example of how language can capture a cross-section of history, culture, and tradition, transforming a simple greeting into a term that encompasses a wide array of meanings and practices over centuries.

Examples:
1275 - Heo fulde hir scale of wine & þus hailede him on. Lauerd king wæs hail. — Laȝamon.

1275 - Þat freond sæiðe to freonde..Leofue freond wæs hail. —
La3amon.

1275 - Rouwenne..bar an hire honde ane guldene bolle. i-uulled mid
wine & þus ærest sæide in Ænglene londe. Lauerd king wæs hæil.
— La3amon.

1300 - Wyn and ale deden he fete, And made[n] hem glade and bliþe,
Wesseyl ledden he fele siþe. — Havelok.

1400 - Odemoun..Toke Menelaus In that swyng, And him bare ouer
his hors tayl: He 3aff him there suche a wassail, That he lay longe
In colde swot. — Laud Troy-bk.

1400 - We3e wyn in þis won 'wassayl!' he cryes. — Cleanness.

1400 - Ronewenne..come wiþ a coupe of golde..and knelede bifore þe
kyng, and saide to him 'Whatsaile!' — Brut.

1494 - When the steward cometh in at the hall doore with the wassell,
he must crie three tymes, Wassell, wassell, wassell. — Coll.
Ordinances Royal Househ.

1548 - Then was the wassaill or banket brought in, and so brake vp
Christmas. — Hall's Vnion: Henry VIII.

1569 - I trust this wassall shall make all England glad. And with that
he dranke a great draught, the king pledging him. — R. Grafton.

1598 - A wassaile on twelfe night. — E. Guilpin.

1601 - And even at this day [in Spain] in their great feasts..they have a
certaine Wassaile or Bragat, which goeth round about the table,
made of honied wine or sweet mead, with..hearbes in it. — P.
Holland.

1603 - The king doth wake to night, & takes his rowse, Keepe wassel.
— Shakespeare.

1607 - Haue you done your wassayl, tis a handsome drowsie dittie Ile
assure yee, now I had as leeue here a Catte cry. — F. Beaumont.

1612 - I see a custome in some parts among vs,..I meane the yearely was-haile in the country on the vigil of the New yeare. — J. Selden.

1614 - I sweare,..By Cresus name and by his castle, Where winter nights he keepeth wassell. — R. Tailor.

1616 - The iolly wassall walkes the often round, And in their cups, their cares are drown'd. — B. Jonson.

1623 - His two Chamberlaines Will I with Wine, and Wassell, so conuince, That Memorie..shall be a Fume. — Shakespeare.

1643 - Ha. What? who goes there? Moth. Waes heal thou gentle Knight. — W. Cartwright.

1650 - Good Dame here at your Door Our Wassel we begin. — New Christmas Carols.

1658 - Wassail,..an ancient Ceremonious custome, still used upon twelf day at night, of going about with a great bowl of Ale, drinking of healths. — E. Phillips.

1661 - For a King of our Wassell this night we must chuse. — New Carolls for Christmas.

1689 - The Pope in sending Rellicks to Princes, does as Wenches do by their Wassels at New-years-tide, they present you with a Cup, and you must drink of a slabby stuff; but the meaning is, you must give them Moneys. — R. Milward.

1742–50 - 'Bove all things else he Wassel priz'd and ale. — R. O. Cambridge.

1805 - The blithesome signs of wassel gay Decayed not with the dying day. — Scott.

1808 - On Christmas eve..The wassel round, in good brown bowls Garnish'd with ribbons, blithely trowls. — Scott.

1820 - I at length arrived in merry Eastcheap, that ancient region of wit and wassail. — W. Irving.

1821 - Meantime the lady and her lover sate At wassail in their beauty and their pride. — Byron.

1832 - Then lift the can to bearded lip,..Wassaile! to every dark-ribbed ship, To every battle-field! — W. Motherwell.

1837 - They sat down..to a substantial supper, and a mighty bowl of wassail..in which the hot apples were hissing and bubbling. — Dickens.

1843 - Fair mistress Sybill, your dainty lips will not, I trow, refuse me the waisall. [Another ed. reads waissel.] — E. Bulwer-Lytton.

1850 - Strangely falls our Christmas eve... Let no footstep beat the floor, Nor bowl of wassail mantle warm. — Tennyson.

1863 - The Berserks drank 'Was-hael! To the Lord!' — H. W. Longfellow.

1878 - Two kings held wassail in Orkadàl. — H. Phillips.

1898 - He was much addicted to wine and wassail too, as his blood-red face sufficiently attested.— J. B. Crozier

Forms

Welcome to the Style Workshops – Building Your Literary Muscles:

Listen up, class! We've covered reading like a pro, but now it's time to sharpen those writing skills. You see, writing isn't just stringing words together. It's about choosing the right tools and knowing how to wield them. It's about sculpting sentences, crafting paragraphs, and assembling a structure that hits your readers right where you intend.

You think learning new words is enough? Think again! In this workshop, we're not just flexing vocabulary; we're building whole new forms of sentences. These structures are going to become your new best friends. You'll get to know them, you'll learn to love them, and most importantly, you'll master them.

But don't expect a cakewalk. This is where the rubber meets the road. We'll explore different effects, targeting exactly the reader you want, hitting them with precision. And trust me, this takes work, dedication, and a whole lot of sweat.

Ready to step up your game? Grab your pen, roll up your sleeves, and let's dive into these style workshops. Your words are your weights, your sentences are your sets, and this workshop? It's your literary gym. Let's build those muscles![2]

---

[2] Some of these examples and ideas have been taken from *A Rhetoric of Pleasure* by T.R. Johnson, *Writing Well* by Donald Hall, and *Quick Takes* by Elizabeth Penfield and Theodora Hill. I have worked to modify them to make them unique for my readers. All readers are advised to look there for more help in writing well.

Style Workshop #1: Clarity – Cutting Through the Fog

Hold onto your hats, wordsmiths, because clarity is where the action starts. Clarity isn't about playing it safe. It's about striking hard, striking true, and leaving no room for misinterpretation. Let's get down to brass tacks:

---

1. Red Riding Hood Revisited:

Compare these two sentences:

- Once upon a time, a walk through the woods by Little Red Riding Hood was occurring when a jump-out from behind a tree by the Big Bad Wolf caused fright in her.
- Once upon a time, Little Red Riding Hood was walking through the woods, when the Big Bad Wolf jumped out from behind a tree and frightened her.

Feel the difference? The second one is lean, mean, and gets to the point. No dancing around with extra words. It foregrounds character and action. Now, do the same with this mouthful:

- The loss of market share to Japan by American automobile manufacturers resulted in the loss of employment by hundreds of thousands of factory workers in Detroit and a decline in the general economy of the upper Midwest.

Clear the fog, focus on character and action, and rewrite that sentence!

---

2. Devices That Aid in Clarity:

- Distinctio: You think abstract words like "beautiful" or "evil" are clear? Make them crystal! Specify what you mean. Here's how:
  Example: It is impossible to make gasoline that costs five cents a gallon—by impossible I mean currently beyond our technological abilities.
  Your turn: Ben Affleck is a versatile actor. Clarify "versatile" with a distinctio!
- Exemplum: Need to explain a complex concept? Paint a picture with words. Like this:
  Example: The conifers (evergreens like pine and cypress trees) produce seeds in hard, cone-shaped structures.
  Now describe a whale to someone who didn't grow up near the ocean using exemplum.
- Amplification: Make those words sing! Describe something ordinary, like ice cream, in extraordinary detail:
  Example: In my hunger after ten days of overly rigorous dieting, I saw visions of ice cream—mountains of creamy, luscious, vanilla ice cream, dripping with gooey hot fudge syrup and many millions of calories.
  Use amplification to describe a freshman's joy or terror during a month-long winter break at her parents' house.
- Metanoia: Mid-sentence revision, changing course, and hitting the mark. It's like conversational jazz:
  Example: The most important aspect of a tenor saxophone's reed is its solidity; no, not its solidity so much as its inner strength. You certainly don't want one that's brittle.
  Now, use metanoia to express how you might feel just before your in-laws come to your house for dinner.

That's the drill, students. Dig deep, cut through the jargon, and make those words dance. Don't just write; communicate! And remember, clarity isn't just about simplicity; it's about precision, force, and impact. Now, get to work!

Style Workshop #2: Emphasis and Syntax – Power and Precision

Welcome back, literary athletes! Did you enjoy the taste of clarity? Ready for something a bit more complex? Emphasis and syntax are your gym equipment here. We're going to stretch those writing muscles to give your sentences not just clarity but rhythm, resonance, and power.

Buckle up, and let's dive into the devices:

---

1. Devices That Aid in Emphasis:

- Asyndeton: Skip those conjunctions! Create a feeling of overflow and energy. Compare these examples:

  When he came home from the war, the government held a grand ceremony, decorating him with medals, ribbons, titles, and riches.

  When he came home from the war, the government held a grand ceremony, decorating him with medals, ribbons, titles, riches.

  Now, unleash the asyndeton to detail the marvelous luxuries of your Thanksgiving meal when you return home.

- Polysyndeton: Go wild with conjunctions. Slow things down and highlight each detail:

Example: When the police opened the trunk of her car, they found stolen jewelry and loaded guns and high-grade cocaine and suitcases full of thousands of dollars.

Now, describe your last act of egregiously bad behavior with polysyndeton.

- Aporia: Present an intriguing doubt or dilemma. Hook 'em in!

  Example: The question of dress codes is tricky; they can suppress gang insignia but also individuality.

  Your turn: Dilemma! Study for a Monday-morning midterm or celebrate a 21st birthday the night before?

- Anantapodoton: Leave them hanging... in a good way.

  Example: If you kill and eat the alligator you will become a man, but if the alligator kills and eats you . . .

  Now, use anantapodoton with a shopping cart, a roommate, Twitter, a life raft, or beans.

2. Devices That Involve Syntax:

- Zeugma: Link multiple phrases with a common word. It's a chain reaction!
  Example: She grabbed her purse, her gloves, and her car keys.
  Describe your getting-ready routine for an evening out with zeugma.
- Syllepsis: Play with a link word in a witty way. Twist those clichés!
  Example: He lost his heart in San Francisco and his shirt in Las Vegas.
  Use syllepsis with "the end of my rope," "catch a ride," or "eat your words."
- Appositive: Describe a noun with another noun. Precision!
  Example: Mrs. Wilkins, the manager, saw the suspect fleeing.
  Modify "A peanut butter and jelly sandwich" with an appositive.
- Anastrophe: Swap the adjective's position for a delightful twist.
  Example: Phoebe displayed an air of confidence unusual for one so young.
  Use anastrophe to describe a dining hall delicacy.

Style Workshop #3: The Art of Transitions – Building Bridges with Words

Well, word artists, are your tools sharpened? Are your literary muscles warmed up? In the world of writing, transitions are the bridges that guide your reader smoothly from one idea to the next. No sudden bumps or jarring turns; it's all about a seamless flow. Let's explore this transition terrain!

Useful Transitional Words and Phrases:

- Similarity: also, and, besides, furthermore, likewise, moreover
- Sequence: after, before, finally, first, later, next
- Contrast: but, however, instead, nevertheless, otherwise, yet
- Cause/Effect: because, consequently, for, hence, therefore
- Emphasis: finally, indeed, nonetheless, still, to summarize, clearly

And this isn't all, creative thinkers! Think "up until now," "in addition to," "meanwhile," "on the other hand," and more. It's a vast bridge network!

Verbal Devices to Master Transitions:

- Procatelpsis: Counter the counterarguments like a debate champion!
  Example: The Beatles' greatness might seem unsurpassable, but with rock n' roll being young, who knows what the future

holds?

Challenge: Use procatelpsis with Justin Beiber and Johnny Cash; a penguin and a monkey; a bathrobe and cowboy boots (and don't start with "Some might say.").

- Hypophora: Ask and answer, a two-step dance of rhetoric.
  Example: How to remove a one-armed English professor from a tree? Wave!
  Task: Craft hypophora about dorm life at Saint Mary's. Be insightful or witty or both!

Anadiplosis: Repeat and link. Build that bridge clause by clause.
Examples: Respect the rules, rules created for your safety.

- A priest's credibility, a credibility respected by all.
  Your turn: Use anadiplosis with Fred Flintstone, Ruffles potato chips, or a chosen athlete, and make it tasty with "taste" or "to taste."

Conduplicatio: Emphasize through repetition. Hammer that point home!
Examples: People adore Scrabble, and indeed, Scrabble's sales show it.

- Some love Scrabble; others liken it to a beating.
  Flex your writing: Create a sentence with conduplicatio and dune buggies, pretzels, umbrellas, or snakes. Bonus if you use them all!

There you have it, aspiring word-smiths! Transitions are your road signs, your bridges, your guiding stars. They take your reader by the hand and lead them on a delightful, unexpected journey through your thoughts. Never underestimate the connective power of a well-placed "however" or a clever use of anadiplosis. Now, take these tools and build your bridges. Write on, warriors of words!

Style Workshop #4: The Grand Game of FIGURATIVE LANGUAGE

In the era of the European Renaissance, a literary training camp was established for young scholars where they had to learn and practice 180 different plays of figurative language. This might seem like an overburdened playbook by today's standards, given that we often "score goals," "fumble," "throw a Hail Mary," "train hard," and "start a new season" without a second thought. (Unfortunately, these figurative phrases have become the equivalent of outdated training drills.)

Figurative language can be divided into two major leagues: tropes, which execute a change in the typical playbook; and schemes, which arrange the players in unique formations.

TROPES: The Offensive Plays

Metaphor: A Power Play

Example: Post-midterms, my brain is a depleted field.

> Coaching Tip: Your imagery should outmatch the subject, just like a powerhouse team. "The river's flow embraced the earth like a tender hug" isn't as striking because a hug isn't as grand as a river's flow.

Simile: A Precision Pass

Example: The over-fertilized tree's leaves looked like overcooked stadium hot dogs.

Coaching Tip: Aim your simile like a well-timed pass. "Consider the body's immune system as a team's defense" works better than "A team's defense is like the body's immune system."

Analogy: A Complex Game Plan

Example: One Hundred and Twenty-fifth Street to Harlem is what the baseline is to basketball, a constant, dynamic presence.

Coaching Tip: Ensure that your analogy isn't a failed trick play. Comparing old books to worn-out jerseys doesn't quite fit as books still serve a purpose, unlike worn-out jerseys.

Antonomasia: The Nickname Game

Example: "His Airness" (Michael Jordan), "The Iron Lady" (Margaret Thatcher), or calling a clumsy teammate "Butterfingers."

SCHEMES: The Defensive Strategies

Parallelism: A Well-Drilled Defense

Examples: We play. That may be the heart of the game. But we coach. That may be the essence of our legacy. If you want to shoot like Steph Curry, you have to train like Steph Curry.

Anaphora: A Repeated Defensive Stance

Example: They kept running, fearing the rival's pursuit, fearing the loss, fearing the coach's wrath.

Inverted Word Order: A Surprise Play

Example: Quick and agile it was not; but intimidating—the sumo wrestler was.

Reversed Structure: The Counterattack

Example: Don't ask what your team can do for you; ask what you can do for your team.

Renaissance students were like athletes, running drills using all 180 figures of speech, creating connected game strategies. Here's your challenge: create a match report using the following plays based on the theme of your high school graduation game:

- metaphor
- simile
- analogy
- antonomasia (offensive or defensive)
- parallelism
- inverted word order
- anaphora
- reversed structure

Each play must stand out on its own, demonstrating your best tactics. Avoid the predictable and keep your fans engaged with fresh plays.

The Sound of the Game: Crowd Cheers and Jeers

Alliteration: The repetitive cheer of the fans.
- "He hits hard, he hits fast!"

Assonance: The harmonious hum of the home crowd.
- "Go, go, go for gold!"

Consonance: The clashing cymbals of the band.
- "Beat, beat, beat the heat!"

Onomatopoeia: The sounds that mirror the action.
- "Swish!" "Whack!" "Boom!"

The Game's Tone: Playing Smoothly or Roughly

Euphony: The grace of a perfect play.
- As when the balletic dribble dances down the court.

Cacophony: The collision of a fierce tackle.
- As in the crunch of helmets in a hard-fought football match.

Remember, the playing field of language is both thrilling and treacherous. Keep your plays fresh, avoid those worn-out drills, and always strive to engage your fans with unexpected twists and turns on the court of prose. The game of language awaits!

The Playing Field of Punctuation: Game Strategies for Writers

Team, huddle up! Writing is a sport of the mind, and like any great game, it has rules, strategies, and skills that we must master. In the stadium of sentences, punctuation marks are the plays that guide our way. They're the tactics that take the words from the starting line to the end zone. Let's break down the playbook, using sports analogies to understand these mighty markers!

THE COMMA: The Timeout

Comma in action: "Unsure of other responses, they take a picture."

A comma is the timeout in a sentence. It tells the reader to pause momentarily before moving on. Just as a coach calls a timeout to regroup the players, a comma gathers your thoughts, helping you pace your reading.

THE COLON: The Two-Minute Warning

Colon in play: "Her life story consists of one triumph after another: victories at every stage of life."

A colon is like the two-minute warning in football. It signals that something significant is about to follow, much like the crucial moments at the end of a half when every play counts.

THE SEMICOLON: The Halftime

Semicolon play: "His fly is undone; the toilet seat is broken."

A semicolon is the halftime of a sentence. It's a more substantial pause that separates two main plays or thoughts, yet still keeps them in the same game, linking related ideas.

THE DASH: The Fast Break

Dash on the field: "The aroma of an orange—this is it!—and the skillful slicing of it."

A dash is like a fast break in basketball. It injects energy and motion into the sentence, allowing a sudden change of direction or an exciting interruption.

PARENTHESES, QUOTATION MARKS, EXCLAMATION POINT: The Playbook, The Commentary, The Victory Shout

Parentheses: play directions, Quotation marks: the coach's words, Exclamation point: the triumph.

These are the playbook (guidelines), the commentary ("spoken words"), and the victory shout (excitement!). They guide, explain, and emphasize, creating the rhythm, tone, and excitement of the game.

A METAPHOR FOR A PARAGRAPH: The Game Quarter

Consider a paragraph as a quarter in a football game. Each sentence is a play, and coherence is the game plan. Revise the scene below to follow this game plan, as if captured by the cameras.

Let's see some examples of how the above can be deployed to improve student writing.

Example Paragraph 1: The Commas and Semicolons Play

Before:

"Although the team won the game, the coach was not satisfied with their performance they lacked cohesion and failed to execute their plays; their victory was a result of the opponent's mistakes not their skill."

After:

"Although the team won the game, the coach was not satisfied with their performance; they lacked cohesion and failed to execute their plays. Their victory was a result of the opponent's mistakes, not their skill."

Explanation: Here, the revised paragraph uses a semicolon to create a halftime between two related thoughts, and commas for smaller timeouts to separate clauses, aligning with the game plan of the comma and semicolon strategies.

Example Paragraph 2: The Dash and Parentheses Playbook

Before:

"The star player who was suffering from a nagging injury he still managed to score the game-winning goal a goal that was an inspiration to his teammates."

After:

"The star player—who was suffering from a nagging injury—still managed to score the game-winning goal (a goal that was an inspiration to his teammates)."

Explanation: The revised paragraph uses dashes to execute a fast break, creating an energetic interruption, and parentheses to add play directions, adding clarity to the game of the sentence.

Example Paragraph 3: The Colon and Paragraph Strategy

Before:

"The season's stats are impressive the leading scorer has 30 goals, the defense has allowed the fewest goals in the league and the goalkeeper has 10 shutouts. The team is now poised to win the championship. The training regimen has been intense. The fans are excited."

After:

"The season's stats are impressive: the leading scorer has 30 goals, the defense has allowed the fewest goals in the league, and the goalkeeper has 10 shutouts. The team is now poised to win the championship. The training regimen has been intense. The fans are excited."

Explanation: This paragraph employs a colon like a two-minute warning, signaling that an important list is about to follow. Additionally, the coherence is improved, aligning the sentences like a well-coordinated game quarter, showing the game plan as the team moves closer to the championship.

By implementing the advice in these revised paragraphs, the text flows more naturally and coherently, mirroring the rhythm and excitement of a well-played game.

Many writers talk about Flow and Focus but few know what it is. The below paragraphs are failures. Can you figure out why?

FLOW

Many astonishing questions about the nature of the universe have been raised by scientists exploring black holes in space. The collapse of a dead star into a point perhaps no larger than an acorn creates a black hole. So much matter pressed into so little volume changes the fabric of space around it in confusing ways. My favorite movie of all time, Interstellar, actually deals with the issues surrounding black holes.

FOCUS

Kenosha, Wisconsin, is the snowmobile capital of America. The
buzzing of snowmobile engines fills the air, and their tank-like tracks
criss-cross the snow. The snow reminds me of Dad's mashed
potatoes, covered with furrows I would draw with my fork. Dad's
mashed potatoes usually made me sick, that's why I was playing with
them. I like to make a hole in the middle of the potatoes and fill it
with gravy. This behavior often made my little sister laugh. But,
really, making my little sister laugh isn't very hard. She laughs at
everything, because she's crazy.

Peer Review:

The Game Plan for Writing Success

Writing, much like sports, is a competitive field where success requires practice, strategy, and teamwork. While I may not stand on the sidelines during a game, as a mentor in the world of writing, I want to share a game plan for refining your craft. This strategy is centered around peer review, and here's how it translates into the language of sports:

1. Facing the Hard Truths: Training Camp for Writers

In sports, athletes face rigorous training sessions where weaknesses are exposed and addressed. Likewise, peer review is the training camp for writers. It involves accepting hard truths about where your writing might falter and needs improvement.

No champion athlete avoids drills that expose their weaknesses, and no writer should avoid honest feedback. Remember, every defeat contains a secret—the secret to the next victory.

2. The Balance of Encouragement and Criticism: The Coach's Talk

Every great coach knows that molding a winning player involves a delicate balance of criticism and encouragement. In the realm of writing, peer review requires the same balance.

Feedback should be precise, highlighting where the work falls short, but it must also be motivating, pointing out strengths and showing faith in the writer's ability to improve. It's like a halftime pep talk that inspires the team to come back stronger in the second half.

3. Embracing the Growth Mindset: Training to Win

A growth mindset is as essential in writing as it is in sports. Athletes train relentlessly, learning from every game, every practice, every play. Writers must approach peer review with the same attitude.

Accepting criticism, learning from it, and using it to fuel growth is akin to an athlete's daily training routine. It's about progressing, enhancing skills, and constantly moving toward that championship win.

Conclusion: Writing as a Competitive Sport

Writing may not take place on a field or court, but it's a competitive sport in its own right. Success requires strategy, practice, and the willingness to learn from both victories and defeats.

Peer review is a vital part of the writer's training regimen. It's the practice session, the game analysis, the coach's guidance, all rolled into one. It's about honing your skills, accepting the challenges, and pushing for excellence.

So, whether you're a novice writer or a seasoned pro, embrace peer review as if you're training for the biggest game of your life. Keep in mind that the point of any game, even the game of writing, is to win. Utilize your teammates, learn from your defeats, and keep pushing for that championship title. In writing, as in sports, the pursuit of excellence never ends.

Questions to help you review one another's work

- Strengths and Weaknesses: Identify 3 major strengths of this paper. What's hitting the mark? Now, spot 3 weak points. Where is the writer fumbling? Be precise, like analyzing game footage.
- Best and Worst Plays: Point out the strongest paragraph. Why's it scoring? Now find the weakest one. What's causing the miss?
- Stumbles and Fumbles: Did you stumble over any sentences, having to reread them to grasp the meaning? Highlight at least one. Treat it like a play that went wrong; we need to correct it.
- Transitions - Offensive and Defensive: Which transitions guide you smoothly down the field of thought? Which ones are blocking your path? Identify the moves that work and those that don't.
- The Final Whistle - Conclusion: What's happening in the conclusion? Is it summarizing the plays? Reflecting on the game's implications? Or throwing a curveball with a new idea? How's it affecting your reading game?

- Questions for the Quarterback - The Writer: What questions are you left with for the writer? What do you need to understand their game plan better?
- Lessons for Your Own Game: What has this paper taught you about your own playbook? What will you start or stop doing in your writing game?
- Understanding the Game Plan - The Thesis: Restate the thesis in your own words. Struggling to find it? Explain why it's eluding you.
- Taking the Field - Writer's Position: What's the writer's stance in this paper? What argument are they laying out on the field?
- Key Plays - Evidence: List the three most vital pieces of evidence or support. Which point scores a touchdown, and which one's dropping the ball? Why?
- Tactics - Author's Methods: Consider the writer's game tactics. Which methods are clear, and which plays are still hidden in the fog?
- Data Highlights - The Winning Stats: What are the 2-3 critical data points driving this argument? They're the stats that make or break the game. Identify them.

Remember, team, this peer review is your practice session for the big game. It's not about being easy on each other; it's about pushing each other to victory. Let's approach it with the same tenacity and precision we'd take to the field. The goal here isn't merely to play; it's to win. Let's make champions out of each other!

Please write a response to your peer's papers addressing the points above. No need to cover all of these questions and there may be issues you need to point out in the paper which are not covered here.

Close Reading

A Guide to Closer Reading – Your Literary Workout

Step 1: Observe the Text – Warm Up Your Mind:

Alright, class, let's begin by flexing those intellectual muscles. In observing the text, you're not just reading – you're seeing what lies on the page. You're examining the bare bones, the inarguable facts. Think of it as a mental stretch, noting every detail. Here's your checklist:

- Repetition: Does anything repeat?
- Grammar: How are sentences constructed?
- Adjectives/Descriptors: What's being described, and how?
- People: Who are the characters?
- Dialogue: What's being said?
- Environment/Location: Where are things happening?
- Repetition: Does anything repeat?
- Cause/Effect: What leads to what?
- Formatting: How are lines, stanzas, etc., arranged?
- Time: When is this happening?
- Comparison/Contrast: What's being compared or contrasted?

Scribble on it, underline, make it your own. But remember, no detail is too small. Ask yourself the basic questions: Who, What, When, Where, Why, How? You're letting the text speak, and you're listening.

Step 2: Plant the Seeds – Questions Are Your Friends:

Now that you've taken a good look, let's start planting those seeds of interpretation. What words baffle you? Which parts need more exploring? What's that relationship between the cell phone and the compact? All these observations are your soil, and those questions are the seeds you're planting. They may seem small, but they're the beginnings of something bigger. They're what will lead you to truly grasp the meaning.

Step 3: Dig Deeper – Context and Content, Together:

With your list of questions, you're ready to dig deeper. Yes, it's going to get tougher, but that's where the real growth happens. Answer those questions from the text, see how the context fits in, but always be aware of when you're bringing in outside knowledge. That's your shovel – use it wisely.

Step 4: Building Understanding – The Heavy Lifting:

Now you're getting to the core. The motivation, the feelings, the structure – what's really driving this text? Why is it shaped this way? You're lifting the heavy weights here, class, but you're strong enough to do it. This is where your effort starts to pay off.

Step 5: Interpretation – The Final Sprint:

You're almost there. You've observed, questioned, dug deep, and built understanding. Now it's time for that final sprint. Take everything you've learned, and form it into a coherent interpretation of the text. What's it all about? What's it trying to tell you? Put that into a few paragraphs. Explain your process, show your work. This isn't just an exercise – it's a full-fledged literary workout, and you've conquered it.

And remember, class – no shortcuts! Just like in the gym, you only get out what you put in. Dig deep, think hard, and let the text speak to you. You've got this! Next we will try out our close reading skills on some short poems. I have chosen fair use publicly available poems by Thomas Traherne (my favorite!) but feel free to try out these techniques on any short piece of writing you like.

The Ways Of Wisdom

*"Her ways are ways of pleasantness, and all her paths
    are peace."*

These sweeter far than lilies are,
No roses may with these compare!
        How these excel,
            No tongue can tell,
Which he that well and truly knows
        With praise and joy he goes!
How great and happy's he that knows his ways
        To be divine and heavenly Joys:
To whom each city is more brave
Than walls of pearl and streets which gold doth pave:
        Whose open eyes
            Behold the skies;
Who loves their wealth and beauty more
        Than kings love golden ore!
Who sees the heavenly ancient ways
Of God the Lord with joy and praise,
        More than the skies
            With open eyes
Doth prize them all; yea, more than gems,
        And regal diadems;
That more esteemeth mountains, as they are,
    Than if they gold and silver were:
To whom the sun more pleasure brings
Than crowns and thrones and palaces to kings:
        That knows his ways
            To be the joys
And way of God—those things who knows
        With joy and praise he goes!

91

Walking

To walk abroad is, not with eyes,
But thoughts, the fields to see and prize;
Else may the silent feet,
Like logs of wood,
Move up and down, and see no good
Nor joy nor glory meet.

Ev'n carts and wheels their place do change,
But cannot see, though very strange
The glory that is by;
Dead puppets may
Move in the bright and glorious day,
Yet not behold the sky.

And are not men than they more blind,
Who having eyes yet never find
The bliss in which they move;
Like statues dead
They up and down are carried
Yet never see nor love.

To walk is by a thought to go;
To move in spirit to and fro;
To mind the good we see;
To taste the sweet;
Observing all the things we meet
How choice and rich they be.

To note the beauty of the day,

And golden fields of corn survey;
Admire each pretty flow'r
With its sweet smell;
To praise their Maker, and to tell
The marks of his great pow'r.

To fly abroad like active bees,
Among the hedges and the trees,
To cull the dew that lies
On ev'ry blade,
From ev'ry blossom; till we lade
Our minds, as they their thighs.

Observe those rich and glorious things,
The rivers, meadows, woods, and springs,
The fructifying sun;
To note from far
The rising of each twinkling star
For us his race to run.

A little child these well perceives,
Who, tumbling in green grass and leaves,
May rich as kings be thought,
But there's a sight
Which perfect manhood may delight,
To which we shall be brought.

While in those pleasant paths we talk,
'Tis that tow'rds which at last we walk;
For we may by degrees
Wisely proceed

Pleasures of love and praise to heed,
From viewing herbs and trees.

A Serious and Pathetical Contemplation of the Mercies of God

> *For all the mysteries, engines, instruments, wherewith
> the world is filled, which we are able to frame and use
> to thy glory.*

For all the trades, variety of operations, cities, temples, streets,
bridges, mariner's compass, admirable picture, sculpture, writing,
printing, songs and music; wherewith the world is beautified and
adorned.
Much more for the regent life,
And power of perception,
Which rules within.
That secret depth of fathomless consideration
That receives the information
Of all our senses,
That makes our centre equal to the heavens,
And comprehendeth in itself the magnitude of the world;
The involv'd mysteries
Of our common sense;
The inaccessible secret
Of perceptive fancy;
The repository and treasury
Of things that are past;
The presentation of things to come;
Thy name be glorified
For evermore.

O miracle
Of divine goodness!

O fire! O flame of zeal, and love, and joy!
Ev'n for our earthly bodies, hast thou created all things.
{ visible
All things { material
{ sensible
Animals,
Vegetables,
Minerals,
Bodies celestial,
Bodies terrestrial,
The four elements,
Volatile spirits,
Trees, herbs, and flowers,
The influences of heaven,
Clouds, vapors, wind,
Dew, rain, hail and snow,
Light and darkness, night and day,
The seasons of the year.
Springs, rivers, fountains, oceans,
Gold, silver, and precious stones.
Corn, wine, and oil,
The sun, moon, and stars,
Cities, nations, kingdoms.
And the bodies of men, the greatest treasures of all,
For each other.
What then, O Lord, hast thou intended for our
Souls, who givest to our bodies such glorious things!

Shadows in the Water

In unexperienced infancy
Many a sweet mistake doth lie:
Mistake though false, intending true;
A seeming somewhat more than view;
    That doth instruct the mind
    In things that lie behind,
And many secrets to us show
Which afterwards we come to know.

Thus did I by the water's brink
Another world beneath me think;
And while the lofty spacious skies
Reversèd there, abused mine eyes,
    I fancied other feet
    Came mine to touch or meet;
As by some puddle I did play
Another world within it lay.

Beneath the water people drowned,
Yet with another heaven crowned,
In spacious regions seemed to go
As freely moving to and fro:
    In bright and open space
    I saw their very face;
Eyes, hands, and feet they had like mine;
Another sun did with them shine.

'Twas strange that people there should walk,
And yet I could not hear them talk;
That through a little watery chink,
Which one dry ox or horse might drink,
    We other worlds should see,
    Yet not admitted be;
And other confines there behold

Of light and darkness, heat and cold.

I called them oft, but called in vain;
No speeches we could entertain:
Yet did I there expect to find
Some other world, to please my mind.
  I plainly saw by these
  A new antipodes,
Whom, though they were so plainly seen,
A film kept off that stood between.

By walking men's reversèd feet
I chanced another world to meet;
Though it did not to view exceed
A phantom, 'tis a world indeed,
  Where skies beneath us shine,
  And earth by art divine
Another face presents below,
Where people's feet against ours go.

Within the regions of the air,
Compassed about with heavens fair,
Great tracts of land there may be found
Enriched with fields and fertile ground;
  Where many numerous hosts
  In those far distant coasts,
For other great and glorious ends
Inhabit, my yet unknown friends.

O ye that stand upon the brink,
Whom I so near me through the chink
With wonder see: what faces there,
Whose feet, whose bodies, do ye wear?
  I my companions see
  In you, another me.
They seemèd others, but are we;

Our second selves these shadows be.

Look how far off those lower skies
Extend themselves! scarce with mine eyes
I can them reach. O ye my friends,
What secret borders on those ends?
　　　Are lofty heavens hurled
'Bout your inferior world?
Are yet the representatives
Of other peoples' distant lives?

Of all the playmates which I knew
That here I do the image view
In other selves, what can it mean?
But that below the purling stream
　　　Some unknown joys there be
　　　Laid up in store for me;
To which I shall, when that thin skin
Is broken, be admitted in.

Wonder

How like an angel came I down!
How bright are all things here!
When first among his works I did appear
O how their glory me did crown!
The world resembled his eternity,
In which my soul did walk;
And ev'ry thing that I did see
Did with me talk.

The skies in their magnificence,
The lively, lovely air;
Oh how divine, how soft, how sweet, how fair!
The stars did entertain my sense,
And all the works of God, so bright and pure,
So rich and great did seem,
As if they ever must endure
In my esteem.

A native health and innocence
Within my bones did grow,
And while my God did all his glories show,
I felt a vigour in my sense
That was all spirit. I within did flow
With seas of life, like wine;
I nothing in the world did know
But 'twas divine.

Harsh ragged objects were conceal'd,
Oppressions tears and cries,
Sins, griefs, complaints, dissensions, weeping eyes
Were hid, and only things reveal'd
Which heav'nly spirits, and the angels prize.
The state of innocence
And bliss, not trades and poverties,

Did fill my sense.

The streets were pav'd with golden stones,
The boys and girls were mine,
Oh how did all their lovely faces shine!
The sons of men were holy ones,
In joy and beauty they appear'd to me,
And every thing which here I found,
While like an angel I did see,
Adorn'd the ground.

Rich diamond and pearl and gold
In ev'ry place was seen;
Rare splendours, yellow, blue, red, white and green,
Mine eyes did everywhere behold.
Great wonders cloth'd with glory did appear,
Amazement was my bliss,
That and my wealth was ev'ry where:
No joy to this!

Curs'd and devis'd proprieties,
With envy, avarice
And fraud, those fiends that spoil even Paradise,
Flew from the splendour of mine eyes,
And so did hedges, ditches, limits, bounds,
I dream'd not aught of those,
But wander'd over all men's grounds,
And found repose.

Proprieties themselves were mine,
And hedges ornaments;
Walls, boxes, coffers, and their rich contents
Did not divide my joys, but all combine.
Clothes, ribbons, jewels, laces, I esteem'd
My joys by others worn:
For me they all to wear them seem'd

When I was born.

To the Same Purpose

To the same purpose: he, not long before
Brought home from nurse, going to the door
To do some little thing
He must not do within,
With wonder cries,
As in the skies
He saw the moon, "O yonder is the moon,
Newly come after me to town,
That shined at Lugwardin but yesternight,
Where I enjoyed the self-same sight."

As if it had ev'n twenty thousand faces,
It shines at once in many places;
To all the earth so wide
God doth the stars divide,
With so much art
The moon impart,
They serve us all; serve wholly every one
As if they servèd him alone.
While every single person hath such store,
'Tis want of sense that makes us poor.

Eden

A learned and a happy ignorance
      Divided me
      From all the vanity,
From all the sloth, care, pain, and sorrow that advance
      The madness and the misery
Of men. No error, no distraction I
Saw soil the earth, or overcloud the sky.

   I knew not that there was a serpent's sting,
      Whose poison shed
      On men, did overspread
The world; nor did I dream of such a thing
      As sin, in which mankind lay dead.
They all were brisk and living wights to me,
Yea, pure and full of immortality.

   Joy, pleasure, beauty, kindness, glory, love,
      Sleep, day, life, light,
      Peace, melody, my sight,
My ears and heart did fill and freely move.
      All that I saw did me delight.
The Universe was then a world of treasure,
To me an universal world of pleasure.

   Unwelcome penitence was then unknown,
      Vain costly toys,
      Swearing and roaring boys,
Shops, markets, taverns, coaches, were unshown;
      So all things were that drown'd my joys:
No thorns chok'd up my path, nor hid the face
Of bliss and beauty, nor eclips'd the place.

   Only what Adam in his first estate,
      Did I behold;

Hard silver and dry gold
As yet lay under ground; my blessed fate
   Was more acquainted with the old
And innocent delights which he did see
In his original simplicity.

  Those things which first his Eden did adorn,
    My infancy
   Did crown. Simplicity
Was my protection when I first was born.
   Mine eyes those treasures first did see
Which God first made. The first effects of love
My first enjoyments upon earth did prove;

  And were so great, and so divine, so pure;
    So fair and sweet,
   So true; when I did meet
Them here at first, they did my soul allure,
   And drew away my infant feet
Quite from the works of men; that I might see
The glorious wonders of the Deity.

Innocence

But that which most I wonder at, which most
I did esteem my bliss, which most I boast,
And ever shall enjoy, is that within
I felt no stain, nor spot of sin.

No darkness then did overshade,
    But all within was pure and bright,
No guilt did crush, nor fear invade
    But all my soul was full of light.

A joyful sense and purity
    Is all I can remember;
  The very night to me was bright,
    'Twas summer in December.

A serious meditation did employ
My soul within, which taken up with joy
Did seem no outward thing to note, but fly
All objects that do feed the eye.

While it those very objects did
    Admire, and prize, and praise, and love,
Which in their glory most are hid,
    Which presence only doth remove.

    Their constant daily presence I
Rejoicing at, did see;
    And that which takes them from the eye
Of others, offer'd them to me.

No inward inclination did I feel
To avarice or pride: my soul did kneel
In admiration all the day. No lust, nor strife,
Polluted then my infant life.

No fraud nor anger in me mov'd,
    No malice, jealousy, or spite;
All that I saw I truly lov'd.
    Contentment only and delight

    Were in my soul. O Heav'n! what bliss
Did I enjoy and feel!
    What powerful delight did this
Inspire! for this I daily kneel.

Whether it be that nature is so pure,
And custom only vicious; or that sure
God did by miracle the guilt remove,
And make my soul to feel his love

So early: or that 'twas one day,
    Wherein this happiness I found;
Whose strength and brightness so do ray,
    That still it seems me to surround;

What ere it is, it is a light
    So endless unto me
That I a world of true delight
    Did then and to this day do see.

That prospect was the gate of Heav'n, that day
The ancient light of Eden did convey
Into my soul: I was an Adam there
A little Adam in a sphere

Of joys! O there my ravish'd sense
    Was entertain'd in Paradise,
And had a sight of innocence
    Which was beyond all bound and price.

An antepast of Heaven sure!
    I on the earth did reign;
Within, without me, all was pure;
    I must become a child again.

News

News from a foreign country came,
As if my treasures and my joys lay there;
    So much it did my heart inflame,
'Twas wont to call my soul into mine ear;
        Which thither went to meet
          Th' approaching sweet,
        And on the threshold stood
    To entertain the secret good;
        It hover'd there
        As if 'twould leave mine ear,
And was so eager to embrace
Th' expected tidings as they came,
That it could change its dwelling place
      To meet the voice of fame.

    As if new tidings were the things
Which did comprise my wished unknown treasure,
    Or else did bear them on their wings,
With so much joy they came, with so much pleasure,
      My soul stood at the gate
        To recreate
      Itself with bliss, and woo
Its speedier approach; a fuller view
      It fain would take,
      Yet journeys back would make
Unto my heart, as if 'twould fain
Go out to meet, yet stay within,
Fitting a place to entertain
      And bring the tidings in.

    What sacred instinct did inspire
My soul in childhood with an hope so strong?
    What secret force mov'd my desire
T' expect my joys beyond the seas, so young?

Felicity I knew
    Was out of view;
And being left alone,
I thought all happiness was gone
        From earth; for this
    I long'd for absent bliss,
Deeming that sure beyond the seas,
Or else in something near at hand
Which I knew not, since nought did please
    I knew, my bliss did stand.

But little did the infant dream
That all the treasures of the world were by,
    And that himself was so the cream
And crown of all which round about did lie.
        Yet thus it was! The gem,
        The diadem,
    The ring enclosing all
That stood upon this earthen ball;
        The heav'nly eye,
    Much wider than the sky,
Wherein they all included were;
The love, the soul, that was the king
Made to possess them, did appear
    A very little thing.

The Salutation

These little limbs,
     These eyes and hands which here I find,
  These rosy cheeks wherewith my life begins,
     Where have ye been? behind
What curtain were ye from me hid so long?
Where was, in what abyss, my speaking tongue?

     When silent I
  So many thousand, thousand years
Beneath the dust did in a chaos lie,
     How could I smiles or tears,
Or lips or hands or eyes or ears perceive?
Welcome ye treasures which I now receive.

     I that so long
  Was nothing from eternity,
Did little think such joys as ear or tongue
     To celebrate or see:
Such sounds to hear, such hands to feel, such feet,
Beneath the skies on such a ground to meet.

     New burnished joys,
  Which yellow gold and pearls excel!
Such sacred treasures are the limbs in boys,
     In which a soul doth dwell;
Their organizèd joints and azure veins
More wealth include than all the world contains.

     From dust I rise,
  And out of nothing now awake;
These brighter regions which salute mine eyes,
     A gift from God I take.
The earth, the seas, the light, the day, the skies,
The sun and stars are mine if those I prize.

Long time before
I in my mother's womb was born,
A God, preparing, did this glorious store,
The world, for me adorn.
Into this Eden so divine and fair,
So wide and bright, I come His son and heir.

A stranger here
Strange things doth meet, strange glories see;
Strange treasures lodged in this fair world appear,
Strange all and new to me;
But that they mine should be, who nothing was,
That strangest is of all, yet brought to pass.

Now that we have exercised our close reading muscles on some smaller texts we are ready to exercise them on something a little longer. Let's look at the end of the Jowett translation of Plato's Phaedrus. In this scene Socrates and Phaedrus are deep in a discussion, let's see how it ends and practice our close reading skills on it.

SOCRATES: I have heard a tradition of the ancients, whether true or not they only know; although if we had found the truth ourselves, do you think that we should care much about the opinions of men?
PHAEDRUS: Your question needs no answer; but I wish that you would tell me what you say that you have heard.
SOCRATES: At the Egyptian city of Naucratis, there was a famous old god, whose name was Theuth; the bird which is called the Ibis is sacred to him, and he was the inventor of many arts, such as arithmetic and calculation and geometry and astronomy and draughts and dice, but his great discovery was the use of letters. Now in those days the god Thamus was the king of the whole country of Egypt; and he dwelt in that great city of Upper Egypt which the Hellenes call Egyptian Thebes, and the god himself is called by them Ammon. To him came Theuth and showed his inventions, desiring that the other Egyptians might be allowed to have the benefit of them; he enumerated them, and Thamus enquired about their several uses, and praised some of them and censured others, as he approved or disapproved of them. It would take a long time to repeat all that Thamus said to Theuth in praise or blame of the various arts. But when they came to letters, This, said Theuth, will make the Egyptians wiser and give them better memories; it is a specific both for the memory and for the wit. Thamus replied: O most ingenious Theuth, the parent or inventor of an art is not always the best judge of the

utility or inutility of his own inventions to the users of them. And in this instance, you who are the father of letters, from a paternal love of your own children have been led to attribute to them a quality which they cannot have; for this discovery of yours will create forgetfulness in the learners' souls, because they will not use their memories; they will trust to the external written characters and not remember of themselves. The specific which you have discovered is an aid not to memory, but to reminiscence, and you give your disciples not truth, but only the semblance of truth; they will be hearers of many things and will have learned nothing; they will appear to be omniscient and will generally know nothing; they will be tiresome company, having the show of wisdom without the reality.

PHAEDRUS: Yes, Socrates, you can easily invent tales of Egypt, or of any other country.

SOCRATES: There was a tradition in the temple of Dodona that oaks first gave prophetic utterances. The men of old, unlike in their simplicity to young philosophy, deemed that if they heard the truth even from 'oak or rock,' it was enough for them; whereas you seem to consider not whether a thing is or is not true, but who the speaker is and from what country the tale comes.

PHAEDRUS: I acknowledge the justice of your rebuke; and I think that the Theban is right in his view about letters.

SOCRATES: He would be a very simple person, and quite a stranger to the oracles of Thamus or Ammon, who should leave in writing or receive in writing any art under the idea that the written word would be intelligible or certain; or who deemed that writing was at all better than knowledge and recollection of the same matters?

PHAEDRUS: That is most true.

SOCRATES: I cannot help feeling, Phaedrus, that writing is unfortunately like painting; for the creations of the painter have the attitude of life, and yet if you ask them a question they preserve a solemn silence. And the same may be said of speeches. You would imagine that they had intelligence, but if you want to know anything and put a question to one of them, the speaker always gives one unvarying answer. And when they have been once written down they are tumbled about anywhere among those who may or may not understand them, and know not to whom they should reply, to whom not: and, if they are maltreated or abused, they have no parent to protect them; and they cannot protect or defend themselves.

PHAEDRUS: That again is most true.

SOCRATES: Is there not another kind of word or speech far better than this, and having far greater power—a son of the same family, but lawfully begotten?

PHAEDRUS: Whom do you mean, and what is his origin?

SOCRATES: I mean an intelligent word graven in the soul of the learner, which can defend itself, and knows when to speak and when to be silent.

PHAEDRUS: You mean the living word of knowledge which has a soul, and of which the written word is properly no more than an image?

SOCRATES: Yes, of course that is what I mean. And now may I be allowed to ask you a question: Would a husbandman, who is a man of sense, take the seeds, which he values and which he wishes to bear fruit, and in sober seriousness plant them during the heat of summer, in some garden of Adonis, that he may rejoice when he sees them in eight days appearing in beauty? at least he would do so, if at all, only for the sake of amusement and pastime. But when he is in earnest he sows in fitting soil, and practices husbandry, and is satisfied if in eight months the seeds which he has sown arrive at perfection?

PHAEDRUS: Yes, Socrates, that will be his way when he is in earnest; he will do the other, as you say, only in play.

SOCRATES: And can we suppose that he who knows the just and good and honorable has less understanding, than the husbandman, about his own seeds?

PHAEDRUS: Certainly not.

SOCRATES: Then he will not seriously incline to 'write' his thoughts 'in water' with pen and ink, sowing words which can neither speak for themselves nor teach the truth adequately to others?

PHAEDRUS: No, that is not likely.

SOCRATES: No, that is not likely—in the garden of letters he will sow and plant, but only for the sake of recreation and amusement; he will write them down as memorials to be treasured against the forgetfulness of old age, by himself, or by any other old man who is treading the same path. He will rejoice in beholding their tender growth; and while others are refreshing their souls with banqueting and the like, this will be the pastime in which his days are spent.

PHAEDRUS: A pastime, Socrates, as noble as the other is ignoble, the pastime of a man who can be amused by serious talk, and can discourse merrily about justice and the like.

SOCRATES: True, Phaedrus. But nobler far is the serious pursuit of the dialectician, who, finding a congenial soul, by the help of science sows and plants therein words which are able to help themselves and him who planted them, and are not unfruitful, but have in them a seed which others brought up in different soils render immortal, making the possessors of it happy to the utmost extent of human happiness.

PHAEDRUS: Far nobler, certainly.

SOCRATES: And now, Phaedrus, having agreed upon the premises we may decide about the conclusion.

PHAEDRUS: About what conclusion?

SOCRATES: About Lysias, whom we censured, and his art of writing, and his discourses, and the rhetorical skill or want of skill which was shown in them—these are the questions which we sought to determine, and they brought us to this point. And I think that we are now pretty well informed about the nature of art and its opposite.

PHAEDRUS: Yes, I think with you; but I wish that you would repeat what was said.

SOCRATES: Until a man knows the truth of the several particulars of which he is writing or speaking, and is able to define them as they are, and having defined them again to divide them until they can be no longer divided, and until in like manner he is able to discern the nature of the soul, and discover the different modes of discourse which are adapted to different natures, and to arrange and dispose them in such a way that the simple form of speech may be addressed to the simpler nature, and the complex and composite to the more complex nature—until he has accomplished all this, he will be unable to handle arguments according to rules of art, as far as their nature allows them to be subjected to art, either for the purpose of teaching or persuading;—such is the view which is implied in the whole preceding argument.

PHAEDRUS: Yes, that was our view, certainly.

SOCRATES: Secondly, as to the censure which was passed on the speaking or writing of discourses, and how they might be rightly or wrongly censured—did not our previous argument show—?

PHAEDRUS: Show what?

SOCRATES: That whether Lysias or any other writer that ever was or will be, whether private man or statesman, proposes laws and so becomes the author of a political treatise, fancying that there is any great certainty and clearness in his performance, the fact of his so writing is only a disgrace to him, whatever men may say. For not to know the nature of justice and injustice, and good and evil, and not to be able to distinguish the dream from the reality, cannot in truth be otherwise than disgraceful to him, even though he have the applause of the whole world.

PHAEDRUS: Certainly.

SOCRATES: But he who thinks that in the written word there is necessarily much which is not serious, and that neither poetry nor prose, spoken or written, is of any great value, if, like the compositions of the rhapsodes, they are only recited in order to be believed, and not with any view to criticism or instruction; and who thinks that even the best of writings are but a reminiscence of what we know, and that only in principles of justice and goodness and nobility taught and communicated orally for the sake of instruction and graven in the soul, which is the true way of writing, is there clearness and perfection and seriousness, and that such principles are a man's own and his legitimate offspring;—being, in the first place, the word which he finds in his own bosom; secondly, the brethren and descendants and relations of his idea which have been duly implanted by him in the souls of others;—and who cares for them and no others—this is the right sort of man; and you and I, Phaedrus, would pray that we may become like him.

PHAEDRUS: That is most assuredly my desire and prayer.

SOCRATES: And now the play is played out; and of rhetoric enough. Go and tell Lysias that to the fountain and school of the Nymphs we went down, and were bidden by them to convey a message to him and to other composers of speeches—to Homer and other writers of poems, whether set to music or not; and to Solon and others who have composed writings in the form of political discourses which they would term laws—to all of them we are to say that if their compositions are based on knowledge of the truth, and they can defend or prove them, when they are put to the test, by spoken arguments, which leave their writings poor in comparison of them, then they are to be called, not only poets, orators, legislators, but are worthy of a higher name, befitting the serious pursuit of their life.

PHAEDRUS: What name would you assign to them?

SOCRATES: Wise, I may not call them; for that is a great name which belongs to God alone,—lovers of wisdom or philosophers is their modest and befitting title.

PHAEDRUS: Very suitable.

SOCRATES: And he who cannot rise above his own compilations and compositions, which he has been long patching and piecing, adding some and taking away some, may be justly called poet or speech-maker or law-maker.

PHAEDRUS: Certainly.

SOCRATES: Now go and tell this to your companion.

PHAEDRUS: But there is also a friend of yours who ought not to be forgotten.

SOCRATES: Who is he?

PHAEDRUS: Isocrates the fair:—What message will you send to him, and how shall we describe him?

SOCRATES: Isocrates is still young, Phaedrus; but I am willing to hazard a prophecy concerning him.

PHAEDRUS: What would you prophesy?

SOCRATES: I think that he has a genius which soars above the orations of Lysias, and that his character is cast in a finer mold. My impression of him is that he will marvelously improve as he grows older, and that all former rhetoricians will be as children in comparison of him. And I believe that he will not be satisfied with rhetoric, but that there is in him a divine inspiration which will lead him to things higher still. For he has an element of philosophy in his nature. This is the message of the gods dwelling in this place, and which I will myself deliver to Isocrates, who is my delight; and do you give the other to Lysias, who is yours.

PHAEDRUS: I will; and now as the heat is abated let us depart.

SOCRATES: Should we not offer up a prayer first of all to the local deities?

PHAEDRUS: By all means.

SOCRATES: Beloved Pan, and all ye other gods who haunt this place, give me beauty in the inward soul; and may the outward and inward man be at one. May I reckon the wise to be the wealthy, and may I have such a quantity of gold as a temperate man and he only can bear and carry.—Anything more? The prayer, I think, is enough for me.

PHAEDRUS: Ask the same for me, for friends should have all things in common.

SOCRATES: Let us go.

What did you notice? Try reading it again and write down whatever questions you have.

Your final activity is to attempt to read something big and hard. For that we will turn to a longer work by Plato. Try to take your time, slow down, and enjoy it!

Gorgias: An Abridged Modernization for Contemporary Writing

By Plato ~380 BC

Translated by Benjamin Jowett

S.P.A.A.

Socrates taught plato

Plato taught aristotle

wrote plays & comedies & tragedies

aristotle taught alexander the great

he conqured the entire world

PERSONS OF THE DIALOGUE:

Callicles
(Cal-eh-clees)

Socrates — Plato's teacher ; philosopher
(Soc.-rat-tees)

Chaerephon

Gorgias — sofist / wise person ; not a philosopher ; good at convincing
(Gor-gee-us)

Polus
(Poll-us)

A Silent Crowd

Setting: The House of Callicles.

rich citizen

Round 1: The Undercard

[handwritten: Old text / Convo (observed)]

[handwritten: uses proverb to sound smarter]

CALLICLES: The wise man, as the proverb says, is late for a fight, but not for a feast.[3] *[handwritten: → feast for eyes]*

SOCRATES: And are we late for a feast?

CALLICLES: Yes, and a delightful feast; for Gorgias has just been demonstrating many fine things to us. *[handwritten: what is he / Sophist]*

SOCRATES: It is not my fault, Callicles; our friend Chaerephon is to blame; for he would keep us loitering in the town square.[4] *[handwritten: looking for clients by showing his wisdom]*

CHAEREPHON: Never mind, Socrates; the misfortune of which I have been the cause I will also repair; for Gorgias is a friend of mine, and I will make him give the demonstration again either now, or, if you prefer, at some other time.

[handwritten left margin: They're late → What does he have to do?]

CALLICLES: What is the matter, Chaerephon—does Socrates want to hear Gorgias?

CHAEREPHON: Yes, that was our intention in coming.

CALLICLES: Come into my house, then; for Gorgias is staying with me, and he shall demonstrate to you.

[handwritten: asks a lot / Why asks of questions]

SOCRATES: Very good, Callicles; but will he answer our questions? for I want to hear from him what is the nature of his art, and what it is which he professes and

---

3 Stephanus Numbers 447-448d

4 The original term for "town square" was "agora" which is the traditional meeting place for large political assemblies as well as an open air market.

teaches; he may, as you (Chaerephon) suggest, defer the demonstration to some other time.

CALLICLES: There is nothing like asking him, Socrates; and indeed to answer questions is a part of his demonstration, for he was saying only just now, that any one in my house might put any question to him, and that he would answer.

SOCRATES: How fortunate! Will you ask him, Chaerephon—?

CHAEREPHON: What shall I ask him?

SOCRATES: Ask him who he is. ⚔

CHAEREPHON: What do you mean?

SOCRATES: I mean such a question as would elicit ? from him, if he had been a maker of shoes, the answer that he is a cobbler. Do you understand?

CHAEREPHON: I understand, and will ask him: Tell me, Gorgias, is our friend Callicles right in saying that you undertake to answer any questions which you are asked?

GORGIAS: Quite right, Chaerephon: I was saying as much only just now; and I may add, that many years have elapsed since anyone has asked me a new one.

CHAEREPHON: Then you must be very ready, Gorgias.

GORGIAS: Of that, Chaerephon, you can try me.

POLUS: Yes, indeed, and if you like, Chaerephon, you may try me too, for I think that Gorgias, who has been talking a long time, is tired.

125

CHAEREPHON: And do you, Polus, think that you can answer better than Gorgias?

POLUS: What does that matter if I answer well enough for you?

CHAEREPHON: Not at all:—and you shall answer if you like.

POLUS: Ask:—

CHAEREPHON: My question is this: If Gorgias had the skill of his brother Herodicus, what ought we to call him? Ought he not to have the name which is given to his brother?

POLUS: Certainly.

CHAEREPHON: Then we should be right in calling him a physician?

POLUS: Yes.

CHAEREPHON: And if he had the skill of Aristophon the son of Aglaophon, or of his brother Polygnotus, what ought we to call him?

POLUS: Clearly, a painter.

CHAEREPHON: But now what shall we call him— what is the art in which he is skilled.

POLUS: O Chaerephon, there are many arts among mankind which are experimental, and have their origin in experience, for experience makes the days of men to proceed according to art, and inexperience according to chance, and different persons in different ways are proficient in different arts, and the best persons in the best arts. And our friend Gorgias is one of the best, and the art in which he is a proficient is the noblest.

what art
↓
could
why is he proficient?

be a philosopher → answers a lot of questions

126

Round 2: The Main Event

SOCRATES: Polus has been taught how to make a capital speech, Gorgias; but he is not fulfilling the promise which he made to Chaerephon.[5]

GORGIAS: What do you mean, Socrates?

SOCRATES: I mean that he has not exactly answered the question which he was asked.

GORGIAS: Then why not ask him yourself?

SOCRATES: But I would much rather ask you, if you are disposed to answer: for I see, from the few words which Polus has uttered, that he has attended more to the art which is called rhetoric than to dialectic.

POLUS: What makes you say so, Socrates?

SOCRATES: Because, Polus, when Chaerephon asked you what was the art which Gorgias knows, you praised it as if you were answering some one who found fault with it, but you never said what the art was.

POLUS: Why, did I not say that it was the noblest of arts?

SOCRATES: Yes, indeed, but that was no answer to the question: nobody asked what was the quality, but what was the nature, of the art, and by what name we were to describe Gorgias. And I would still beg you briefly and clearly, as you answered Chaerephon when he asked you at first, to say what this art is, and what we ought to call Gorgias: Or rather, Gorgias, let me turn to

---

[5] Stephanus Numbers 448d-461b

128

you, and ask the same question,—what are we to call you, and what is the art which you profess?

GORGIAS: Rhetoric, Socrates, is my art. *rhetoric comes up a lot... why?*

SOCRATES: Then I am to call you a rhetorician?

GORGIAS: Yes, Socrates, and a good one too, if you would call me that which, in Homeric language, 'I boast myself to be.'

SOCRATES: I should wish to do so.

GORGIAS: Then pray do.

SOCRATES: And are we to say that you are able to make other men rhetoricians?

GORGIAS: Yes, that is exactly what I profess to make them, not only at Athens, but in all places.

SOCRATES: And will you continue to ask and answer questions, Gorgias, as we are at present doing, and reserve for another occasion the longer mode of speech which Polus was attempting? Will you keep your promise, and answer shortly the questions which are asked of you?

GORGIAS: Some answers, Socrates, are of necessity longer; but I will do my best to make them as short as possible; for a part of my profession is that I can be as short as any one. *what is it*

SOCRATES: That is what is wanted, Gorgias; demonstrate the shorter method now, and the longer one at some other time.

GORGIAS: Well, I will; and you will certainly say, that you never heard a man use fewer words.

SOCRATES: Very good then; as you profess to be a rhetorician, and a maker of rhetoricians, let me ask you, with what is rhetoric concerned: I might ask with what is weaving concerned, and you would reply (would you not?), with the making of garments?

GORGIAS: Yes.

SOCRATES: And music is concerned with the composition of melodies?

GORGIAS: It is.

SOCRATES: By Hermes, Gorgias, I admire the surpassing brevity of your answers.

GORGIAS: Yes, Socrates, I do think myself good at that.

SOCRATES: I am glad to hear it; answer me in like manner about rhetoric: with what is rhetoric concerned?

GORGIAS: With discourse.

SOCRATES: What sort of discourse, Gorgias?—such discourse as would teach the sick under what treatment they might get well?

GORGIAS: No.

SOCRATES: Then rhetoric does not treat of all kinds of discourse?

GORGIAS: Certainly not.

SOCRATES: And yet rhetoric makes men able to speak?

GORGIAS: Yes.

SOCRATES: And to understand that about which they speak?

GORGIAS: Of course.

SOCRATES: But does not the art of medicine, which we were just now mentioning, also make men able to understand and speak about the sick?

GORGIAS: Certainly.

SOCRATES: Then medicine also treats of discourse?

GORGIAS: Yes.

SOCRATES: Of discourse concerning diseases?

GORGIAS: Just so.

SOCRATES: And does not gymnastic also treat of discourse concerning the good or evil condition of the body?

GORGIAS: Very true.

SOCRATES: And the same, Gorgias, is true of the other arts:—all of them treat of discourse concerning the subjects with which they severally have to do.

GORGIAS: Clearly.

SOCRATES: Then why, if you call rhetoric the art which treats of discourse, and all the other arts treat of discourse, do you not call them arts of rhetoric?

GORGIAS: Because, Socrates, the knowledge of the other arts has only to do with some sort of external action, as of the hand; but there is no such action of the hand in rhetoric which works and takes effect only through the medium of discourse. And therefore I am justified in saying that rhetoric treats of discourse.

SOCRATES: I am not sure whether I entirely understand you, but I dare say I shall soon know better;

131

please answer me a question:—you would allow that there are arts?

GORGIAS: Yes.

SOCRATES: As to the arts generally, they are for the most part concerned with doing, and require little or no speaking; in painting, and statuary, and many other arts, the work may proceed in silence; and of such arts I suppose you would say that they do not come within the province of rhetoric.

GORGIAS: You perfectly conceive my meaning, Socrates.

SOCRATES: But there are other arts which work wholly through the medium of language, and require either no action or very little, as, for example, the arts of arithmetic, of calculation, of geometry, and of playing draughts; in some of these speech is pretty nearly co-extensive with action, but in most of them the verbal element is greater—they depend wholly on words for their efficacy and power: and I take your meaning to be that rhetoric is an art of this latter sort?

GORGIAS: Exactly.

SOCRATES: And yet I do not believe that you really mean to call any of these arts rhetoric; although the precise expression which you used was, that rhetoric is an art which works and takes effect only through the medium of discourse; and an adversary who wished to be captious might say, 'And so, Gorgias, you call arithmetic rhetoric.' But I do not think that you really call arithmetic rhetoric any more than geometry would be so called by you.

GORGIAS: You are quite right, Socrates, in your apprehension of my meaning.

SOCRATES: Well, then, let me now have the rest of my answer:—seeing that rhetoric is one of those arts which works mainly by the use of words, and there are other arts which also use words, tell me what is that quality in words with which rhetoric is concerned:— Suppose that a person asks me about some of the arts which I was mentioning just now; he might say, 'Socrates, what is arithmetic?' and I should reply to him, as you replied to me, that arithmetic is one of those arts which take effect through words. And then he would proceed to ask: 'Words about what?' and I should reply, Words about odd and even numbers, and how many there are of each. And if he asked again: 'What is the art of calculation?' I should say, That also is one of the arts which is concerned wholly with words. And if he further said, 'Concerned with what?' I should say, like the clerks in the assembly, 'as aforesaid' of arithmetic, but with a difference, the difference being that the art of calculation considers not only the quantities of odd and even numbers, but also their numerical relations to themselves and to one another. And suppose, again, I were to say that astronomy is only words—he would ask, 'Words about what, Socrates?' and I should answer, that astronomy tells us about the motions of the stars and sun and moon, and their relative swiftness.

GORGIAS: You would be quite right, Socrates.

SOCRATES: And now let us have from you, Gorgias, the truth about rhetoric: which you would admit (would you not?) to be one of those arts which act always and fulfill all their ends through the medium of words?

GORGIAS: True.

SOCRATES: Words which do what? I should ask. To what class of things do the words which rhetoric uses relate?

GORGIAS: To the greatest, Socrates, and the best of human things.

SOCRATES: That again, Gorgias, is ambiguous; I am still in the dark: for which are the greatest and best of human things? I dare say that you have heard men singing at feasts the old drinking song, in which the singers enumerate the goods of life, first health, beauty next, thirdly, as the writer of the song says, wealth honestly obtained.

GORGIAS: Yes, I know the song; but what is your drift?

SOCRATES: I mean to say, that the producers of those things which the author of the song praises, that is to say, the physician, the trainer, the money-maker, will at once come to you, and first the physician will say: 'O Socrates, Gorgias is deceiving you, for my art is concerned with the greatest good of men and not his.' And when I ask, Who are you? he will reply, 'I am a physician.' What do you mean? I shall say. Do you mean that your art produces the greatest good? 'Certainly,' he will answer, 'for is not health the greatest good? What greater good can men have, Socrates?' And after him the trainer will come and say, 'I too, Socrates, shall be greatly surprised if Gorgias can show more good of his art than I can show of mine.' To him again I shall say, Who are you, honest friend, and what is your business? 'I am a trainer,' he will reply, 'and my business is to make men beautiful and strong in body.' When I have done with the trainer, there arrives the money-maker, and he, as I expect, will utterly despise them all. 'Consider Socrates,' he will say, 'whether Gorgias or any one else can produce any greater good than wealth.' Well, you and I say to him, and are you a creator of wealth? 'Yes,' he replies. And who are you? 'A money-maker.' And do you consider wealth to be the greatest good of man? 'Of course,' will be his reply. And we shall rejoin: Yes; but our friend Gorgias contends that his art produces a greater good than yours. And then he will be sure to go on and ask, 'What good? Let Gorgias answer.' Now I want you, Gorgias, to imagine that this question is asked of you by them and by me; What is that which, as you say, is the greatest good of man, and of which you are the creator? Answer us.

GORGIAS: That good, Socrates, which is truly the greatest, being that which gives to men freedom in their own persons, and to individuals the power of ruling over others in their several states.

SOCRATES: And what would you consider this to be?

GORGIAS: What is there greater than the word which persuades the judges in the courts, or the senators in the council, or the citizens in the assembly, or at any other political meeting?—if you have the power of uttering this word, you will have the physician your slave, and the trainer your slave, and the money-maker

135

of whom you talk will be found to gather treasures, not for himself, but for you who are able to speak and to persuade the multitude.

SOCRATES: Now I think, Gorgias, that you have very accurately explained what you conceive to be the art of rhetoric; and you mean to say, if I am not mistaken, that rhetoric is the artificer of persuasion, having this and no other business, and that this is her crown and end. Do you know any other effect of rhetoric over and above that of producing persuasion?

GORGIAS: No: the definition seems to me very fair, Socrates; for persuasion is the chief end of rhetoric.

SOCRATES: Then hear me, Gorgias, for I am quite sure that if there ever was a man who entered on the discussion of a matter from a pure love of knowing the truth, I am such a one, and I should say the same of you.

GORGIAS: What is coming, Socrates?

SOCRATES: I will tell you: I am very well aware that I do not know what, according to you, is the exact nature, or what are the topics of that persuasion of which you speak, and which is given by rhetoric; although I have a suspicion about both the one and the other. And I am going to ask—what is this power of persuasion which is given by rhetoric, and about what? But why, if I have a suspicion, do I ask instead of telling you? Not for your sake, but in order that the argument may proceed in such a manner as is most likely to set forth the truth. And I would have you observe, that I am right in asking this further question: If I asked, 'What sort of a painter is Zeuxis?' and you said, 'The painter of figures,' should I not be right in asking, 'What kind of figures, and where do you find them?'

GORGIAS: Certainly.

SOCRATES: And the reason for asking this second question would be, that there are other painters besides, who paint many other figures?

GORGIAS: True.

SOCRATES: But if there had been no one but Zeuxis who painted them, then you would have answered very well?

GORGIAS: Quite so.

SOCRATES: Now I want to know about rhetoric in the same way;—is rhetoric the only art which brings persuasion, or do other arts have the same effect? I mean to say—Does he who teaches anything persuade men of that which he teaches or not?

GORGIAS: He persuades, Socrates,—there can be no mistake about that.

SOCRATES: Again, if we take the arts of which we were just now speaking:—do not arithmetic and the arithmeticians teach us the properties of number?

GORGIAS: Certainly.

SOCRATES: And therefore persuade us of them?

GORGIAS: Yes.

SOCRATES: Then arithmetic as well as rhetoric is an artificer of persuasion?

GORGIAS: Clearly.

SOCRATES: And if any one asks us what sort of persuasion, and about what,—we shall answer, persuasion which teaches the quantity of odd and even; and we shall be able to show that all the other arts of which we were just now speaking are artificers of persuasion, and of what sort, and about what.

GORGIAS: Very true.

SOCRATES: Then rhetoric is not the only artificer of persuasion?

GORGIAS: True.

SOCRATES: Seeing, then, that not only rhetoric works by persuasion, but that other arts do the same, as in the case of the painter, a question has arisen which is a very fair one: Of what persuasion is rhetoric the artificer, and about what?—is not that a fair way of putting the question?

GORGIAS: I think so.

SOCRATES: Then, if you approve the question, Gorgias, what is the answer?

GORGIAS: I answer, Socrates, that rhetoric is the art of persuasion in courts of law and other assemblies, as I was just now saying, and about the just and unjust.

SOCRATES: And that, Gorgias, was what I was suspecting to be your notion; yet I would not have you wonder if by-and-by I am found repeating a seemingly plain question; for I ask not in order to confute you, but as I was saying that the argument may proceed consecutively, and that we may not get the habit of anticipating and suspecting the meaning of one another's words; I would have you develop your own views in your own way, whatever may be your hypothesis.

GORGIAS: I think that you are quite right, Socrates.

SOCRATES: Then let me raise another question; there is such a thing as 'having learned'?

GORGIAS: Yes.

SOCRATES: And there is also 'having believed'?

GORGIAS: Yes.

SOCRATES: And is the 'having learned' the same as 'having believed,' and are learning and belief the same things?

GORGIAS: In my judgment, Socrates, they are not the same.

SOCRATES: And your judgment is right, as you may ascertain in this way:—If a person were to say to you, 'Is there, Gorgias, a false belief as well as a true?'—you would reply, if I am not mistaken, that there is.

GORGIAS: Yes.

SOCRATES: Well, but is there a false knowledge as well as a true?

GORGIAS: No.

SOCRATES: No, indeed; and this again proves that knowledge and belief differ.

GORGIAS: Very true.

SOCRATES: And yet those who have learned as well as those who have believed are persuaded?

GORGIAS: Just so.

SOCRATES: Shall we then assume two sorts of persuasion,—one which is the source of belief without knowledge, as the other is of knowledge?

GORGIAS: By all means.

SOCRATES: And which sort of persuasion does rhetoric create in courts of law and other assemblies about the just and unjust, the sort of persuasion which gives belief without knowledge, or that which gives knowledge?

GORGIAS: Clearly, Socrates, that which only gives belief.

SOCRATES: Then rhetoric, as would appear, is the artificer of a persuasion which creates belief about the just and unjust, but gives no instruction about them?

GORGIAS: True.

SOCRATES: And the rhetorician does not instruct the courts of law or other assemblies about things just and unjust, but he creates belief about them; for no one can be supposed to instruct such a vast multitude about such high matters in a short time?

GORGIAS: Certainly not.

SOCRATES: Come, then, and let us see what we really mean about rhetoric; for I do not know what my own meaning is as yet. When the assembly meets to elect a physician or a shipwright or any other craftsman, will the rhetorician be taken into counsel? Surely not. For at every election he ought to be chosen who is most skilled; and, again, when walls have to be built or harbors or docks to be constructed, not the rhetorician but the master workman will advise; or when generals have to be chosen and an order of battle arranged, or a position taken, then the military will advise and not the rhetoricians: what do you say, Gorgias? Since you profess to be a rhetorician and a maker of rhetoricians, I cannot do better than learn the nature of your art from you. And here let me assure you that I have your interest in view as well as my own. For likely enough some one or other of the young men present might desire to become your pupil, and in fact I see some, and a good many too, who have this wish, but they would be too modest to question you. And therefore when you are interrogated by me, I would have you imagine that you are interrogated by them. 'What is the use of coming to you, Gorgias?' they will say—'about what will you teach us to advise the state?—about the just and unjust only, or about those other things also which Socrates has just mentioned?' How will you answer them?

GORGIAS: I like your way of leading us on, Socrates, and I will endeavor to reveal to you the whole nature of rhetoric. You must have heard, I think, that the docks and the walls of the Athenians and the plan of the harbor were devised in accordance with the counsels, partly of Themistocles, and partly of Pericles, and not at the suggestion of the builders.

SOCRATES: Such is the tradition, Gorgias, about Themistocles; and I myself heard the speech of Pericles when he advised us about the middle wall.

GORGIAS: And you will observe, Socrates, that when a decision has to be given in such matters the rhetoricians are the advisers; they are the men who win their point.

SOCRATES: I had that in my admiring mind, Gorgias, when I asked what is the nature of rhetoric, which always appears to me, when I look at the matter in this way, to be a marvel of greatness.

GORGIAS: A marvel, indeed, Socrates, if you only knew how rhetoric comprehends and holds under her sway all the inferior arts. Let me offer you a striking example of this. On several occasions I have been with my brother Herodicus or some other physician to see one of his patients, who would not allow the physician to give him medicine, or apply the knife or hot iron to him; and I have persuaded him to do for me what he would not do for the physician just by the use of rhetoric. And I say that if a rhetorician and a physician were to go to any city, and had there to argue in the Ecclesia or any other assembly as to which of them should be elected state-physician, the physician would have no chance; but he who could speak would be chosen if he wished; and in a contest with a man of any other profession the rhetorician more than any one would have the power of getting himself chosen, for he can speak more persuasively to the multitude than any of them, and on any subject. Such is the nature and power of the art of rhetoric! And yet, Socrates, rhetoric should be used like any other competitive art, not against everybody,—the rhetorician ought not to abuse his strength any more than a boxer or wrestler or other MMA fighter;—because he has powers which are more than a match either for friend or enemy, he ought not therefore to strike, stab,

142

or slay his friends. Suppose a man to have been trained in the palestra and to be a skillful boxer,—he in the fulness of his strength goes and strikes his father or mother or one of his familiars or friends; but that is no reason why the trainers or fencing-masters should be held in detestation or banished from the city;—surely not. For they taught their art for a good purpose, to be used against enemies and evil-doers, in self-defense not in aggression, and others have perverted their instructions, and turned to a bad use their own strength and skill. But not on this account are the teachers bad, neither is the art in fault, or bad in itself; I should rather say that those who make a bad use of the art are to blame. And the same argument holds good of rhetoric; for the rhetorician can speak against all men and upon any subject,—in short, he can persuade the multitude better than any other man of anything which he pleases, but he should not therefore seek to defraud the physician or any other artist of his reputation merely because he has the power; he ought to use rhetoric fairly, as he would also use his athletic powers. And if after having become a rhetorician he makes a bad use of his strength and skill, his instructor surely ought not on that account to be held in detestation or banished. For he was intended by his teacher to make a good use of his instructions, but he abuses them. And therefore he is the person who ought to be held in detestation, banished, and put to death, and not his instructor.

SOCRATES: You, Gorgias, like myself, have had great experience of disputations, and you must have observed, I think, that they do not always terminate in mutual edification, or in the definition by either party of the subjects which they are discussing; but disagreements are apt to arise—somebody says that another has not spoken truly or clearly; and then they get into a passion and begin to quarrel, both parties conceiving that their opponents are arguing from personal feeling only and jealousy of themselves, not from any interest in the question at issue. And sometimes they will go on abusing one another until the company at last are quite vexed at themselves for ever listening to such fellows. Why do I say this? Why, because I cannot help feeling that you are now saying what is not quite consistent or accordant with what you were saying at first about rhetoric. And I am afraid to point this out to you, lest you should think that I have some animosity against you, and that I speak, not for the sake of discovering the truth, but from jealousy of you. Now if you are one of my sort, I should like to cross-examine you, but if not I will let you alone. And what is my sort? you will ask. I am one of those who are very willing to be refuted if I say anything which is not true, and very willing to refute any one else who says what is not true, and quite as ready to be refuted as to refute; for I hold that this is the greater gain of the two, just as the gain is greater of being cured of a very great evil than of curing another. For I imagine that there is no evil which a man can endure so great as an erroneous opinion about the matters of which we are speaking; and if you claim to be one of my sort, let us have the discussion out, but if you would rather have done, no matter;—let us make an end of it.

GORGIAS: I should say, Socrates, that I am quite the man whom you indicate; but, perhaps, we ought to consider the audience, for, before you came, I had already given a long demonstration, and if we proceed the argument may run on to a great length. And therefore I think that we should consider whether we may not be detaining some part of the company when they are wanting to do something else.

CHAEREPHON: You hear the audience cheering, Gorgias and Socrates, which shows their desire to listen to you; and for myself, Heaven forbid that I should have any business on hand which would take me away from a discussion so interesting and so ably maintained.

CALLICLES: By the gods, Chaerephon, although I have been present at many discussions, I doubt whether I was ever so much delighted before, and therefore if you go on discoursing all day I shall be the better pleased.

SOCRATES: I may truly say, Callicles, that I am willing, if Gorgias is.

GORGIAS: After all this, Socrates, I should be disgraced if I refused, especially as I have promised to answer all comers; in accordance with the wishes of the company, then, do you begin, and ask of me any question which you like.

SOCRATES: Let me tell you then, Gorgias, what surprises me in your words; though I dare say that you may be right, and I may have misunderstood your meaning. You say that you can make any man, who will learn of you, a rhetorician?

GORGIAS: Yes.

SOCRATES: Do you mean that you will teach him to gain the ears of the multitude on any subject, and this not by instruction but by persuasion?

GORGIAS: Quite so.

SOCRATES: You were saying, in fact, that the rhetorician will have greater powers of persuasion than the physician even in a matter of health?

GORGIAS: Yes, with the multitude,—that is.

SOCRATES: You mean to say, with the ignorant; for with those who know he cannot be supposed to have greater powers of persuasion.

GORGIAS: Very true.

SOCRATES: But if he is to have more power of persuasion than the physician, he will have greater power than he who knows?

GORGIAS: Certainly.

SOCRATES: Although he is not a physician:—is he?

GORGIAS: No.

SOCRATES: And he who is not a physician must, obviously, be ignorant of what the physician knows.

GORGIAS: Clearly.

SOCRATES: Then, when the rhetorician is more persuasive than the physician, the ignorant is more persuasive with the ignorant than he who has knowledge?—is not that the inference?

GORGIAS: In the case supposed:—yes.

SOCRATES: And the same holds of the relation of rhetoric to all the other arts; the rhetorician need not know the truth about things; he has only to discover some way of persuading the ignorant that he has more knowledge than those who know?

GORGIAS: Yes, Socrates, and is not this a great comfort?—not to have learned the other arts, but the art of rhetoric only, and yet to be in no way inferior to the professors of them?

SOCRATES: Whether the rhetorician is or not inferior on this account is a question which we will hereafter examine if the enquiry is likely to be of any service to us; but I would rather begin by asking, whether he is or is not as ignorant of the just and unjust, base and honorable, good and evil, as he is of medicine and the other arts; I mean to say, does he really know anything of what is good and evil, base or honorable, just or unjust in them; or has he only a way with the ignorant of persuading them that he not knowing is to be esteemed to know more about these things than some one else who knows? Or must the pupil know these things and come to you knowing them before he can acquire the art of rhetoric? If he is ignorant, you who are the teacher of rhetoric will not teach him—it is not your business; but you will make him seem to the multitude to know them, when he does not know them; and seem to be a good man, when he is not. Or will you be unable to teach him rhetoric at all, unless he knows the truth of these things first? What is to be said about all this? By heavens, Gorgias, I wish that you would reveal to me the power of rhetoric, as you were saying that you would.

GORGIAS: Well, Socrates, I suppose that if the pupil does chance not to know them, he will have to learn of me these things as well.

SOCRATES: Say no more, for there you are right; and so he whom you make a rhetorician must either know the nature of the just and unjust already, or he must be taught by you.

GORGIAS: Certainly.

SOCRATES: Well, and is not he who has learned carpentering a carpenter?

GORGIAS: Yes.

SOCRATES: And he who has learned music a musician?

GORGIAS: Yes.

SOCRATES: And he who has learned medicine is a physician, in like manner? He who has learned anything whatever is that which his knowledge makes him.

GORGIAS: Certainly.

SOCRATES: And in the same way, he who has learned what is just is just?

GORGIAS: To be sure.

SOCRATES: And he who is just may be supposed to do what is just?

GORGIAS: Yes.

SOCRATES: And must not the just man always desire to do what is just?

GORGIAS: That is clearly the inference.

SOCRATES: Surely, then, the just man will never consent to do injustice?

GORGIAS: Certainly not.

SOCRATES: And according to the argument the rhetorician must be a just man?

GORGIAS: Yes.

SOCRATES: And will therefore never be willing to do injustice?

GORGIAS: Clearly not.

SOCRATES: But do you remember saying just now that the trainer is not to be accused or banished if the pugilist makes a wrong use of his pugilistic art; and in like manner, if the rhetorician makes a bad and unjust use of his rhetoric, that is not to be laid to the charge of his teacher, who is not to be banished, but the wrong-doer himself who made a bad use of his rhetoric—he is to be banished—was not that said?

GORGIAS: Yes, it was.

SOCRATES: But now we are affirming that the aforesaid rhetorician will never have done injustice at all?

GORGIAS: True.

SOCRATES: And at the very outset, Gorgias, it was said that rhetoric treated of discourse, not (like arithmetic) about odd and even, but about just and unjust? Was not this said?

GORGIAS: Yes.

SOCRATES: I was thinking at the time, when I heard you saying so, that rhetoric, which is always discoursing about justice, could not possibly be an unjust thing. But when you added, shortly afterwards, that the rhetorician might make a bad use of rhetoric I noted with surprise the inconsistency into which you had fallen; and I said, that if you thought, as I did, that there was a gain in being refuted, there would be an advantage in going on with the question, but if not, I would leave off. And in the course of our investigations, as you will see yourself, the rhetorician has been acknowledged to be incapable of making an unjust use of rhetoric, or of willingness to do injustice. By the dog, Gorgias, there will be a great deal of discussion, before we get at the truth of all this.

Round 3: The Colt Fights Back

POLUS: And do even you, Socrates, seriously believe what you are now saying about rhetoric? What! Because Gorgias was ashamed to deny that the rhetorician knew the just and the honorable and the good, and admitted that to any one who came to him ignorant of them he could teach them, and then out of this admission there arose a contradiction—the thing which you dearly love, and to which not he, but you, brought the argument by your captious questions—(do you seriously believe that there is any truth in all this?) For will any one ever acknowledge that he does not know, or cannot teach, the nature of justice? The truth is, that there is great want of manners in bringing the argument to such a pass.[6]

SOCRATES: Illustrious Polus, the reason why we provide ourselves with friends and children is, that when we get old and stumble, a younger generation may be at hand to set us on our legs again in our words and in our actions: and now, if I and Gorgias are stumbling, here are you who should raise us up; and I for my part engage to retract any error into which you may think that I have fallen-upon one condition:

POLUS: What condition?

SOCRATES: That you contract, Polus, the prolixity of speech in which you indulged at first.

---

[6] Stephanus Numbers 461b-481b

POLUS: What! do you mean that I may not use as many words as I please?

SOCRATES: Only to think, my friend, that having come on a visit to Athens, which is the most free-spoken state in Hellas, you when you got there, and you alone, should be deprived of the power of speech—that would be hard indeed. But then consider my case:—shall not I be very hardly used, if, when you are making a long oration, and refusing to answer what you are asked, I am compelled to stay and listen to you, and may not go away? I say rather, if you have a real interest in the argument, or, to repeat my former expression, have any desire to set it on its legs, take back any statement which you please; and in your turn ask and answer, like myself and Gorgias—refute and be refuted: for I suppose that you would claim to know what Gorgias knows—would you not?

POLUS: Yes.

SOCRATES: And you, like him, invite any one to ask you about anything which he pleases, and you will know how to answer him?

POLUS: To be sure.

SOCRATES: And now, which will you do, ask or answer?

POLUS: I will ask; and do you answer me, Socrates, the same question which Gorgias, as you suppose, is unable to answer: What is rhetoric?

SOCRATES: Do you mean what sort of an art?

POLUS: Yes.

SOCRATES: To say the truth, Polus, it is not an art at all, in my opinion.

POLUS: Then what, in your opinion, is rhetoric?

SOCRATES: A thing which, as I was lately reading in a book of yours, you say that you have made an art.

POLUS: What thing?

SOCRATES: I should say a sort of experience.

POLUS: Does rhetoric seem to you to be an experience?

SOCRATES: That is my view, but you may be of another mind.

POLUS: An experience in what?

SOCRATES: An experience in producing a sort of delight and gratification.

POLUS: And if able to gratify others, must not rhetoric be a fine thing?

SOCRATES: What are you saying, Polus? Why do you ask me whether rhetoric is a fine thing or not, when I have not as yet told you what rhetoric is?

POLUS: Did I not hear you say that rhetoric was a sort of experience?

SOCRATES: Will you, who are so desirous to gratify others, afford a slight gratification to me?

POLUS: I will.

SOCRATES: Will you ask me, what sort of an art is cookery?

POLUS: What sort of an art is cookery?

SOCRATES: Not an art at all, Polus.

POLUS: What then?

SOCRATES: I should say an experience.

POLUS: In what? I wish that you would explain to me.

SOCRATES: An experience in producing a sort of delight and gratification, Polus.

POLUS: Then are cookery and rhetoric the same?

SOCRATES: No, they are only different parts of the same profession.

POLUS: Of what profession?

SOCRATES: I am afraid that the truth may seem discourteous; and I hesitate to answer, lest Gorgias should imagine that I am making fun of his own profession. For whether or no this is that art of rhetoric which Gorgias practices I really cannot tell:—from what he was just now saying, nothing appeared of what he thought of his art, but the rhetoric which I mean is a part of a not very creditable whole.

GORGIAS: A part of what, Socrates? Say what you mean, and never mind me.

SOCRATES: In my opinion then, Gorgias, the whole of which rhetoric is a part is not an art at all, but the habit of a bold and ready wit, which knows how to manage mankind: this habit I sum up under the word 'flattery'; and it appears to me to have many other parts, one of which is cookery, which may seem to be an art, but, as I maintain, is only an experience or routine and not an art:—another part is rhetoric, and the art of attiring and sophistry are two others: thus there are four

154

branches, and four different things answering to them. And Polus may ask, if he likes, for he has not as yet been informed, what part of flattery is rhetoric: he did not see that I had not yet answered him when he proceeded to ask a further question: Whether I do not think rhetoric a fine thing? But I shall not tell him whether rhetoric is a fine thing or not, until I have first answered, 'What is rhetoric?' For that would not be right, Polus; but I shall be happy to answer, if you will ask me, What part of flattery is rhetoric?

POLUS: I will ask and do you answer? What part of flattery is rhetoric?

SOCRATES: Will you understand my answer? Rhetoric, according to my view, is the ghost or counterfeit of a part of politics.

POLUS: And noble or ignoble?

SOCRATES: Ignoble, I should say, if I am compelled to answer, for I call what is bad ignoble: though I doubt whether you understand what I was saying before.

GORGIAS: Indeed, Socrates, I cannot say that I understand myself.

SOCRATES: I do not wonder, Gorgias; for I have not as yet explained myself, and our friend Polus, colt by name and colt by nature, is apt to run away.7

GORGIAS: Never mind him, but explain to me what you mean by saying that rhetoric is the counterfeit of a part of politics.

---

7 This is an untranslatable play on the name 'Polus,' which means 'a colt.'

SOCRATES: I will try, then, to explain my notion of rhetoric, and if I am mistaken, my friend Polus shall refute me. We may assume the existence of bodies and of souls?

GORGIAS: Of course.

SOCRATES: You would further admit that there is a good condition of either of them?

GORGIAS: Yes.

SOCRATES: Which condition may not be really good, but good only in appearance? I mean to say, that there are many persons who appear to be in good health, and whom only a physician or trainer will discern at first sight not to be in good health.

GORGIAS: True.

SOCRATES: And this applies not only to the body, but also to the soul: in either there may be that which gives the appearance of health and not the reality?

GORGIAS: Yes, certainly.

SOCRATES: And now I will endeavor to explain to you more clearly what I mean: The soul and body being two, have two arts corresponding to them: there is the art of politics attending on the soul; and another art attending on the body, of which I know no single name, but which may be described as having two divisions, one of them gymnastic, and the other medicine. And in politics there is a legislative part, which answers to gymnastic, as justice does to medicine; and the two parts run into one another, justice having to do with the same subject as legislation, and medicine with the same subject as gymnastic, but with a difference. Now, seeing that there are these four arts, two attending on the body and two on the soul for their highest good; flattery knowing, or rather guessing their natures, has distributed herself into four shams or simulations of them; she puts on the likeness of some one or other of them, and pretends to be that which she simulates, and having no regard for men's highest interests, is ever making pleasure the bait of the unwary, and deceiving them into the belief that she is of the highest value to them. Cookery simulates the disguise of medicine, and pretends to know what food is the best for the body; and if the physician and the cook had to enter into a competition in which children were the judges, or men who had no more sense than children, as to which of them best understands the goodness or badness of food, the physician would be starved to death. A flattery I deem this to be and of an ignoble sort, Polus, for to you I am now addressing myself, because it aims at pleasure without any thought of the best. An art I do not call it, but only an experience, because it is unable to explain or to give a reason of the nature of its own applications. And I do not call any irrational thing an art; but if you dispute my words, I am prepared to argue in defense of them.

Cookery, then, I maintain to be a flattery which takes the form of medicine; and attiring, in like manner, is a flattery which takes the form of gymnastic, and is knavish, false, ignoble, illiberal, working deceitfully by the help of lines, and colors, and enamels, and garments, and making men affect a spurious beauty to the neglect of the true beauty which is given by gymnastic.

I would rather not be tedious, and therefore I will only say, after the manner of the geometricians (for I think that by this time you will be able to follow):

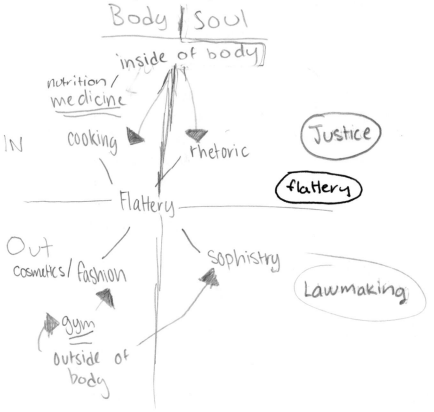

Body | Soul

inside of body

nutrition / medicine

IN

cooking

rhetoric

Justice

flattery

Flattery

Out

cosmetics / fashion

Sophistry

Lawmaking

gym

outside of body

as attiring: gymnastic:: cookery: medicine;

or rather,

as attiring: gymnastic:: sophistry: legislation;

and

as cookery: medicine:: rhetoric: justice.

And this, I say, is the natural difference between the rhetorician and the sophist, but by reason of their near connection, they are apt to be jumbled up together; neither do they know what to make of themselves, nor do other men know what to make of them. For if the body presided over itself, and were not under the guidance of the soul, and the soul did not discern and discriminate between cookery and medicine, but the body was made the judge of them, and the rule of judgment was the bodily delight which was given by them, then the word of Anaxagoras, that word with which you, friend Polus, are so well acquainted, would prevail far and wide: 'Chaos' would come again, and cookery, health, and medicine would mingle in an indiscriminate mass. And now I have told you my notion of rhetoric, which is, in relation to the soul, what cookery is to the body. I may have been inconsistent in making a long speech, when I would not allow you to discourse at length. But I think that I may be excused, because you did not understand me, and could make no use of my answer when I spoke shortly, and therefore I had to enter into an explanation. And if I show an equal inability to make use of yours, I hope that you will speak at equal length; but if I am able to understand you, let me have the benefit of your brevity, as is only fair: And now you may do what you please with my answer.

POLUS: What do you mean? do you think that rhetoric is flattery?

SOCRATES: Nay, I said a part of flattery; if at your age, Polus, you cannot remember, what will you do by-and-by, when you get older?

POLUS: And are the good rhetoricians meanly regarded in states, under the idea that they are flatterers?

SOCRATES: Is that a question or the beginning of a speech?

POLUS: I am asking a question.

SOCRATES: Then my answer is, that they are not regarded at all.

POLUS: How not regarded? Have they not very great power in states?

SOCRATES: Not if you mean to say that power is a good to the possessor.

POLUS: And that is what I do mean to say.

SOCRATES: Then, if so, I think that they have the least power of all the citizens.

POLUS: What! are they not like tyrants? They kill and despoil and exile any one whom they please.

SOCRATES: By the dog, Polus, I cannot make out at each deliverance of yours, whether you are giving an opinion of your own, or asking a question of me.

POLUS: I am asking a question of you.

160

SOCRATES: Yes, my friend, but you ask two questions at once.

POLUS: How two questions?

SOCRATES: Why, did you not say just now that the rhetoricians are like tyrants, and that they kill and despoil or exile any one whom they please?

POLUS: I did.

SOCRATES: Well then, I say to you that here are two questions in one, and I will answer both of them. And I tell you, Polus, that rhetoricians and tyrants have the least possible power in states, as I was just now saying; for they do literally nothing which they will, but only what they think best.

POLUS: And is not that a great power?

SOCRATES: Polus has already said the reverse.

POLUS: Said the reverse! nay, that is what I assert.

SOCRATES: No, by the great—what do you call him? —not you, for you say that power is a good to him who has the power.

POLUS: I do.

SOCRATES: And would you maintain that if a fool does what he thinks best, this is a good, and would you call this great power?

POLUS: I should not.

SOCRATES: Then you must prove that the rhetorician is not a fool, and that rhetoric is an art and not a flattery—and so you will have refuted me; but if you leave me unrefuted, why, the rhetoricians who do what they think best in states, and the tyrants, will have nothing upon which to congratulate themselves, if as you say, power be indeed a good, admitting at the same time that what is done without sense is an evil.

POLUS: Yes; I admit that.

SOCRATES: How then can the rhetoricians or the tyrants have great power in states, unless Polus can refute Socrates, and prove to him that they do as they will?

POLUS: This fellow—

SOCRATES: I say that they do not do as they will;— now refute me.

POLUS: Why, have you not already said that they do as they think best?

SOCRATES: And I say so still.

POLUS: Then surely they do as they will?

SOCRATES: I deny it.

POLUS: But they do what they think best?

SOCRATES: Aye.

POLUS: That, Socrates, is monstrous and absurd.

SOCRATES: Good words, good Polus, as I may say in your own peculiar style; but if you have any questions to ask of me, either prove that I am in error or give the answer yourself.

POLUS: Very well, I am willing to answer that I may know what you mean.

SOCRATES: Do men appear to you to will that which they do, or to will that further end for the sake of which they do a thing? when they take medicine, for example, at the bidding of a physician, do they will the drinking of the medicine which is painful, or the health for the sake of which they drink?

POLUS: Clearly, the health.

SOCRATES: And when men go on a voyage or engage in business, they do not will that which they are doing at the time; for who would desire to take the risk of a voyage or the trouble of business?—But they will, to have the wealth for the sake of which they go on a voyage.

POLUS: Certainly.

SOCRATES: And is not this universally true? If a man does something for the sake of something else, he wills not that which he does, but that for the sake of which he does it.

POLUS: Yes.

SOCRATES: And are not all things either good or evil, or intermediate and indifferent?

POLUS: To be sure, Socrates.

SOCRATES: Wisdom and health and wealth and the like you would call goods, and their opposites evils?

POLUS: I should.

SOCRATES: And the things which are neither good nor evil, and which partake sometimes of the nature of good and at other times of evil, or of neither, are such as sitting, walking, running, sailing; or, again, wood, stones, and the like:—these are the things which you call neither good nor evil?

POLUS: Exactly so.

SOCRATES: Are these indifferent things done for the sake of the good, or the good for the sake of the indifferent?

POLUS: Clearly, the indifferent for the sake of the good.

SOCRATES: When we walk we walk for the sake of the good, and under the idea that it is better to walk, and when we stand we stand equally for the sake of the good?

POLUS: Yes.

SOCRATES: And when we kill a man we kill him or exile him or despoil him of his goods, because, as we think, it will conduce to our good?

POLUS: Certainly.

SOCRATES: Men who do any of these things do them for the sake of the good?

POLUS: Yes.

SOCRATES: And did we not admit that in doing something for the sake of something else, we do not will those things which we do, but that other thing for the sake of which we do them?

POLUS: Most true.

SOCRATES: Then we do not will simply to kill a man or to exile him or to despoil him of his goods, but we will to do that which conduces to our good, and if the act is not conducive to our good we do not will it; for we will, as you say, that which is our good, but that which is neither good nor evil, or simply evil, we do not will. Why are you silent, Polus? Am I not right?

POLUS: You are right.

SOCRATES: Hence we may infer, that if any one, whether he be a tyrant or a rhetorician, kills another or exiles another or deprives him of his property, under the idea that the act is for his own interests when really not for his own interests, he may be said to do what seems best to him?

POLUS: Yes.

SOCRATES: But does he do what he wills if he does what is evil? Why do you not answer?

POLUS: Well, I suppose not.

SOCRATES: Then if great power is a good as you allow, will such a one have great power in a state?

POLUS: He will not.

SOCRATES: Then I was right in saying that a man may do what seems good to him in a state, and not have great power, and not do what he wills?

POLUS: As though you, Socrates, would not like to have the power of doing what seemed good to you in the state, rather than not; you would not be jealous when you saw any one killing or sleeping with or imprisoning whom he pleased, Oh, no!

SOCRATES: Justly or unjustly, do you mean?

POLUS: In either case is he not equally to be envied?

SOCRATES: Forbear, Polus!

POLUS: Why 'forbear'?

SOCRATES: Because you ought not to envy wretches who are not to be envied, but only to pity them.

POLUS: And are those of whom I spoke wretches?

SOCRATES: Yes, certainly they are.

POLUS: And so you think that he who slays any one whom he pleases, and justly slays him, is pitiable and wretched?

SOCRATES: No, I do not say that of him: but neither do I think that he is to be envied.

POLUS: Were you not saying just now that he is wretched?

SOCRATES: Yes, my friend, if he killed another unjustly, in which case he is also to be pitied; and he is not to be envied if he killed him justly.

POLUS: At any rate you will allow that he who is unjustly put to death is wretched, and to be pitied?

SOCRATES: Not so much, Polus, as he who kills him, and not so much as he who is justly killed.

POLUS: How can that be, Socrates?

SOCRATES: That may very well be, inasmuch as doing injustice is the greatest of evils.

POLUS: But is it the greatest? Is not suffering injustice a greater evil?

SOCRATES: Certainly not.

POLUS: Then would you rather suffer than do injustice?

SOCRATES: I should not like either, but if I must choose between them, I would rather suffer than do.

POLUS: Then you would not wish to be a tyrant?

SOCRATES: Not if you mean by tyranny what I mean.

POLUS: I mean, as I said before, the power of doing whatever seems good to you in a state, killing, banishing, doing in all things as you like.

SOCRATES: Well then, illustrious friend, when I have said my say, do you reply to me. Suppose that I go into a crowded town square, and take a dagger under my arm. Polus, I say to you, I have just acquired rare power, and become a tyrant; for if I think that any of these men whom you see ought to be put to death, the man whom I have a mind to kill is as good as dead; and if I am disposed to break his head or tear his garment, he will have his head broken or his garment torn in an instant. Such is my great power in this city. And if you do not believe me, and I show you the dagger, you would probably reply: Socrates, in that sort of way any one may have great power—he may burn any house which he pleases, and the docks and triremes of the Athenians, and all their other vessels, whether public or private— but can you believe that this mere doing as you think best is great power?

POLUS: Certainly not such doing as this.

SOCRATES: But can you tell me why you disapprove of such a power?

POLUS: I can.

SOCRATES: Why then?

POLUS: Why, because he who did as you say would be certain to be punished.

SOCRATES: And punishment is an evil?

POLUS: Certainly.

SOCRATES: And you would admit once more, my good sir, that great power is a benefit to a man if his actions turn out to his advantage, and that this is the meaning of great power; and if not, then his power is an evil and is no power. But let us look at the matter in another way:—do we not acknowledge that the things of which we were speaking, the infliction of death, and exile, and the deprivation of property are sometimes a good and sometimes not a good?

POLUS: Certainly.

SOCRATES: About that you and I may be supposed to agree?

POLUS: Yes.

SOCRATES: Tell me, then, when do you say that they are good and when that they are evil—what principle do you lay down?

POLUS: I would rather, Socrates, that you should answer as well as ask that question.

SOCRATES: Well, Polus, since you would rather have the answer from me, I say that they are good when they are just, and evil when they are unjust.

POLUS: You are hard of refutation, Socrates, but might not a child refute that statement?

SOCRATES: Then I shall be very grateful to the child, and equally grateful to you if you will refute me and deliver me from my foolishness. And I hope that refute me you will, and not weary of doing good to a friend.

POLUS: Yes, Socrates, and I need not go far or appeal to antiquity; events which happened only a few days ago are enough to refute you, and to prove that many men who do wrong are happy.

SOCRATES: What events?

POLUS: You see, I presume, that Archelaus the son of Perdiccas is now the ruler of Macedonia?

SOCRATES: At any rate I hear that he is.

POLUS: And do you think that he is happy or miserable?

SOCRATES: I cannot say, Polus, for I have never had any acquaintance with him.

POLUS: And cannot you tell at once, and without having an acquaintance with him, whether a man is happy?

SOCRATES: Most certainly not.

POLUS: Then clearly, Socrates, you would say that you did not even know whether the great king was a happy man?

SOCRATES: And I should speak the truth; for I do not know how he stands in the matter of education and justice.

POLUS: What! and does all happiness consist in this?

SOCRATES: Yes, indeed, Polus, that is my doctrine; the men and women who are gentle and good are also happy, as I maintain, and the unjust and evil are miserable.

POLUS: Then, according to your doctrine, the said Archelaus is miserable?

SOCRATES: Yes, my friend, if he is wicked.

POLUS: That he is wicked I cannot deny; for he had no title at all to the throne which he now occupies, he being only the son of a woman who was the slave of Alcetas the brother of Perdiccas; he himself therefore in strict right was the slave of Alcetas; and if he had meant to do rightly he would have remained his slave, and then, according to your doctrine, he would have been happy. But now he is unspeakably miserable, for he has been guilty of the greatest crimes: in the first place he invited his uncle and master, Alcetas, to come to him, under the pretense that he would restore to him the throne which Perdiccas has usurped, and after entertaining him and his son Alexander, who was his own cousin, and nearly of an age with him, and making them drunk, he threw them into a waggon and carried them off by night, and slew them, and got both of them out of the way; and when he had done all this wickedness he never discovered that he was the most miserable of all men, and was very far from repenting: shall I tell you how he showed his remorse? He had a younger brother, a child of seven years old, who was the legitimate son of Perdiccas, and to him of right the kingdom belonged; Archelaus, however, had no mind to bring him up as he ought and restore the kingdom to him; that was not his notion of happiness; but not long afterwards he threw him into a well and drowned him, and declared to his mother Cleopatra that he had fallen in while running after a goose, and had been killed. And now as he is the greatest criminal of all the Macedonians, he may be supposed to be the most miserable and not the happiest of them, and I dare say that there are many Athenians, and you would be at the head of them, who would rather be any other Macedonian than Archelaus!

SOCRATES: I praised you at first, Polus, for being a rhetorician rather than a reasoner. And this, as I suppose, is the sort of argument with which you fancy that a child might refute me, and by which I stand refuted when I say that the unjust man is not happy. But, my good friend, where is the refutation? I cannot admit a word which you have been saying.

POLUS: That is because you will not; for you surely must think as I do.

SOCRATES: Not so, my simple friend, but because you will refute me after the manner which rhetoricians practice in courts of law. For there the one party think that they refute the other when they bring forward a number of witnesses of good repute in proof of their allegations, and their adversary has only a single one or none at all. But this kind of proof is of no value where truth is the aim; a man may often be sworn down by a multitude of false witnesses who have a great air of respectability. And in this argument nearly every one, Athenian and stranger alike, would be on your side, if you should bring witnesses in disproof of my statement; —you may, if you will, summon Nicias the son of Niceratus, and let his brothers, who gave the row of tripods which stand in the precincts of Dionysus, come with him; or you may summon Aristocrates, the son of Scellius, who is the giver of that famous offering which is at Delphi; summon, if you will, the whole house of Pericles, or any other great Athenian family whom you choose;—they will all agree with you: I only am left alone and cannot agree, for you do not convince me; although you produce many false witnesses against me, in the hope of depriving me of my inheritance, which is the truth. But I consider that nothing worth speaking of will have been effected by me unless I make you the one witness of my words; nor by you, unless you make me the one witness of yours; no matter about the rest of the world. For there are two ways of refutation, one which is yours and that of the world in general; but mine is of another sort—let us compare them, and see in what they differ. For, indeed, we are at issue about matters which to know is honorable and not to know disgraceful; to know or not to know happiness and misery—that is the chief of them. And what knowledge can be nobler? or what ignorance more disgraceful than this? And therefore I will begin by asking you whether you do not think that a man who is unjust and doing injustice can be happy, seeing that you think Archelaus unjust, and yet happy? May I assume this to be your opinion?

POLUS: Certainly.

SOCRATES: But I say that this is an impossibility—here is one point about which we are at issue:—very good. And do you mean to say also that if he meets with retribution and punishment he will still be happy?

POLUS: Certainly not; in that case he will be most miserable.

SOCRATES: On the other hand, if the unjust be not punished, then, according to you, he will be happy?

POLUS: Yes.

SOCRATES: But in my opinion, Polus, the unjust or doer of unjust actions is miserable in any case,—more miserable, however, if he be not punished and does not meet with retribution, and less miserable if he be punished and meets with retribution at the hands of gods and men.

POLUS: You are maintaining a strange doctrine, Socrates.

SOCRATES: I shall try to make you agree with me, O my friend, for as a friend I regard you. Then these are the points at issue between us—are they not? I was saying that to do is worse than to suffer injustice?

POLUS: Exactly so.

SOCRATES: And you said the opposite?

POLUS: Yes.

SOCRATES: I said also that the wicked are miserable, and you refuted me?

POLUS: By Zeus, I did.

SOCRATES: In your own opinion, Polus.

POLUS: Yes, and I rather suspect that I was in the right.

SOCRATES: You further said that the wrong-doer is happy if he be unpunished?

POLUS: Certainly.

SOCRATES: And I affirm that he is most miserable, and that those who are punished are less miserable—are you going to refute this proposition also?

POLUS: A proposition which is harder of refutation than the other, Socrates.

SOCRATES: Say rather, Polus, impossible; for who can refute the truth?

POLUS: What do you mean? If a man is detected in an unjust attempt to make himself a tyrant, and when detected is racked, mutilated, has his eyes burned out, and after having had all sorts of great injuries inflicted on him, and having seen his wife and children suffer the like, is at last impaled or tarred and burned alive, will he be happier than if he escape and become a tyrant, and continue all through life doing what he likes and holding the reins of government, the envy and admiration both of citizens and strangers? Is that the paradox which, as you say, cannot be refuted?

SOCRATES: There again, noble Polus, you are raising hobgoblins instead of refuting me; just now you were calling witnesses against me. But please to refresh my memory a little; did you say—'in an unjust attempt to make himself a tyrant'?

POLUS: Yes, I did.

SOCRATES: Then I say that neither of them will be happier than the other,—neither he who unjustly acquires a tyranny, nor he who suffers in the attempt, for of two miserables one cannot be the happier, but that he who escapes and becomes a tyrant is the more miserable of the two. Do you laugh, Polus? Well, this is a new kind of refutation,—when any one says anything, instead of refuting him to laugh at him.

POLUS: But do you not think, Socrates, that you have been sufficiently refuted, when you say that which no human being will allow? Ask the company.

SOCRATES: O Polus, I am not a public man, and only last year, when my tribe were serving as Prytanes, and it became my duty as their president to take the votes, there was a laugh at me, because I was unable to take them.[8] And as I failed then, you must not ask me to count the suffrages of the company now; but if, as I was saying, you have no better argument than numbers, let me have a turn, and do you make trial of the sort of proof which, as I think, is required; for I shall produce one witness only of the truth of my words, and he is the person with whom I am arguing; his suffrage I know how to take; but with the many I have nothing to do, and do not even address myself to them. May I ask then whether you will answer in turn and have your words put to the proof? For I certainly think that I and you and every man do really believe, that to do is a greater evil than to suffer injustice: and not to be punished than to be punished.

POLUS: And I should say neither I, nor any man: would you yourself, for example, suffer rather than do injustice?

SOCRATES: Yes, and you, too; I or any man would.

---

[8] Prytanes is the name for the members of the council that runs the city of Athens.

POLUS: Quite the reverse; neither you, nor I, nor any man.

SOCRATES: But will you answer?

POLUS: To be sure, I will; for I am curious to hear what you can have to say.

SOCRATES: Tell me, then, and you will know, and let us suppose that I am beginning at the beginning: which of the two, Polus, in your opinion, is the worst?—to do injustice or to suffer?

POLUS: I should say that suffering was worst.

SOCRATES: And which is the greater disgrace?—Answer.

POLUS: To do.

SOCRATES: And the greater disgrace is the greater evil?

POLUS: Certainly not.

SOCRATES: I understand you to say, if I am not mistaken, that the honorable is not the same as the good, or the disgraceful as the evil?

POLUS: Certainly not.

SOCRATES: Let me ask a question of you: When you speak of beautiful things, such as bodies, colors, figures, sounds, institutions, do you not call them beautiful in reference to some standard: bodies, for example, are beautiful in proportion as they are useful, or as the sight of them gives pleasure to the spectators; can you give any other account of personal beauty?

POLUS: I cannot.

SOCRATES: And you would say of figures or colors generally that they were beautiful, either by reason of the pleasure which they give, or of their use, or of both?

POLUS: Yes, I should.

SOCRATES: And you would call sounds and music beautiful for the same reason?

POLUS: I should.

SOCRATES: Laws and institutions also have no beauty in them except in so far as they are useful or pleasant or both?

POLUS: I think not.

SOCRATES: And may not the same be said of the beauty of knowledge?

POLUS: To be sure, Socrates; and I very much approve of your measuring beauty by the standard of pleasure and utility.

SOCRATES: And deformity or disgrace may be equally measured by the opposite standard of pain and evil?

POLUS: Certainly.

SOCRATES: Then when of two beautiful things one exceeds in beauty, the measure of the excess is to be taken in one or both of these; that is to say, in pleasure or utility or both?

POLUS: Very true.

SOCRATES: And of two deformed things, that which exceeds in deformity or disgrace, exceeds either in pain or evil—must it not be so?

POLUS: Yes.

SOCRATES: But then again, what was the observation which you just now made, about doing and suffering wrong? Did you not say, that suffering wrong was more evil, and doing wrong more disgraceful?

POLUS: I did.

SOCRATES: Then, if doing wrong is more disgraceful than suffering, the more disgraceful must be more painful and must exceed in pain or in evil or both: does not that also follow?

POLUS: Of course.

SOCRATES: First, then, let us consider whether the doing of injustice exceeds the suffering in the consequent pain: Do the injurers suffer more than the injured?

POLUS: No, Socrates; certainly not.

SOCRATES: Then they do not exceed in pain?

POLUS: No.

SOCRATES: But if not in pain, then not in both?

POLUS: Certainly not.

SOCRATES: Then they can only exceed in the other?

POLUS: Yes.

SOCRATES: That is to say, in evil?

POLUS: True.

SOCRATES: Then doing injustice will have an excess of evil, and will therefore be a greater evil than suffering injustice?

POLUS: Clearly.

SOCRATES: But have not you and the world already agreed that to do injustice is more disgraceful than to suffer?

POLUS: Yes.

SOCRATES: And that is now discovered to be more evil?

POLUS: True.

SOCRATES: And would you prefer a greater evil or a greater dishonor to a less one? Answer, Polus, and fear not; for you will come to no harm if you nobly resign yourself into the healing hand of the argument as to a physician without shrinking, and either say 'Yes' or 'No' to me.

POLUS: I should say 'No.'

SOCRATES: Would any other man prefer a greater to a less evil?

POLUS: No, not according to this way of putting the case, Socrates.

SOCRATES: Then I said truly, Polus, that neither you, nor I, nor any man, would rather do than suffer injustice; for to do injustice is the greater evil of the two.

POLUS: That is the conclusion.

SOCRATES: You see, Polus, when you compare the two kinds of refutations, how unlike they are. All men, with the exception of myself, are of your way of thinking; but your single assent and witness are enough for me,—I have no need of any other, I take your suffrage, and am regardless of the rest. Enough of this, and now let us proceed to the next question; which is, Whether the greatest of evils to a guilty man is to suffer punishment, as you supposed, or whether to escape punishment is not a greater evil, as I supposed. Consider:—You would say that to suffer punishment is another name for being justly corrected when you do wrong?

POLUS: I should.

SOCRATES: And would you not allow that all just things are honorable in so far as they are just? Please to reflect, and tell me your opinion.

POLUS: Yes, Socrates, I think that they are.

SOCRATES: Consider again:—Where there is an agent, must there not also be a patient?

POLUS: I should say so.

SOCRATES: And will not the patient suffer that which the agent does, and will not the suffering have the quality of the action? I mean, for example, that if a man strikes, there must be something which is stricken?

POLUS: Yes.

SOCRATES: And if the striker strikes violently or quickly, that which is struck will be struck violently or quickly?

POLUS: True.

SOCRATES: And the suffering to him who is stricken is of the same nature as the act of him who strikes?

POLUS: Yes.

SOCRATES: And if a man burns, there is something which is burned?

POLUS: Certainly.

SOCRATES: And if he burns in excess or so as to cause pain, the thing burned will be burned in the same way?

POLUS: Truly.

SOCRATES: And if he cuts, the same argument holds —there will be something cut?

POLUS: Yes.

SOCRATES: And if the cutting be great or deep or such as will cause pain, the cut will be of the same nature?

POLUS: That is evident.

SOCRATES: Then you would agree generally to the universal proposition which I was just now asserting: that the affection of the patient answers to the affection of the agent?

POLUS: I agree.

SOCRATES: Then, as this is admitted, let me ask whether being punished is suffering or acting?

POLUS: Suffering, Socrates; there can be no doubt of that.

SOCRATES: And suffering implies an agent?

POLUS: Certainly, Socrates; and he is the punisher.

SOCRATES: And he who punishes rightly, punishes justly?

POLUS: Yes.

SOCRATES: And therefore he acts justly?

POLUS: Justly.

SOCRATES: Then he who is punished and suffers retribution, suffers justly?

POLUS: That is evident.

SOCRATES: And that which is just has been admitted to be honorable?

POLUS: Certainly.

SOCRATES: Then the punisher does what is honorable, and the punished suffers what is honorable?

POLUS: True.

SOCRATES: And if what is honorable, then what is good, for the honorable is either pleasant or useful?

POLUS: Certainly.

SOCRATES: Then he who is punished suffers what is good?

POLUS: That is true.

SOCRATES: Then he is benefited?

POLUS: Yes.

SOCRATES: Do I understand you to mean what I mean by the term 'benefited'? I mean, that if he be justly punished his soul is improved.

POLUS: Surely.

SOCRATES: Then he who is punished is delivered from the evil of his soul?

POLUS: Yes.

SOCRATES: And is he not then delivered from the greatest evil? Look at the matter in this way:—In respect of a man's estate, do you see any greater evil than poverty?

POLUS: There is no greater evil.

SOCRATES: Again, in a man's bodily frame, you would say that the evil is weakness and disease and deformity?

POLUS: I should.

SOCRATES: And do you not imagine that the soul likewise has some evil of her own?

POLUS: Of course.

SOCRATES: And this you would call injustice and ignorance and cowardice, and the like?

POLUS: Certainly.

SOCRATES: So then, in mind, body, and estate, which are three, you have pointed out three corresponding evils—injustice, disease, poverty?

POLUS: True.

SOCRATES: And which of the evils is the most disgraceful?—Is not the most disgraceful of them injustice, and in general the evil of the soul?

POLUS: By far the most.

SOCRATES: And if the most disgraceful, then also the worst?

POLUS: What do you mean, Socrates?

SOCRATES: I mean to say, that is most disgraceful has been already admitted to be most painful or hurtful, or both.

POLUS: Certainly.

SOCRATES: And now injustice and all evil in the soul has been admitted by us to be most disgraceful?

POLUS: It has been admitted.

SOCRATES: And most disgraceful either because most painful and causing excessive pain, or most hurtful, or both?

POLUS: Certainly.

SOCRATES: And therefore to be unjust and intemperate, and cowardly and ignorant, is more painful than to be poor and sick?

POLUS: Nay, Socrates; the painfulness does not appear to me to follow from your premises.

SOCRATES: Then, if, as you would argue, not more painful, the evil of the soul is of all evils the most disgraceful; and the excess of disgrace must be caused by some preternatural greatness, or extraordinary hurtfulness of the evil.

POLUS: Clearly.

SOCRATES: And that which exceeds most in hurtfulness will be the greatest of evils?

POLUS: Yes.

SOCRATES: Then injustice and intemperance, and in general the depravity of the soul, are the greatest of evils?

POLUS: That is evident.

SOCRATES: Now, what art is there which delivers us from poverty? Does not the art of making money?

POLUS: Yes.

SOCRATES: And what art frees us from disease? Does not the art of medicine?

POLUS: Very true.

SOCRATES: And what from vice and injustice? If you are not able to answer at once, ask yourself whither we go with the sick, and to whom we take them.

POLUS: To the physicians, Socrates.

SOCRATES: And to whom do we go with the unjust and intemperate?

POLUS: To the judges, you mean.

SOCRATES: —Who are to punish them?

POLUS: Yes.

SOCRATES: And do not those who rightly punish others, punish them in accordance with a certain rule of justice?

POLUS: Clearly.

SOCRATES: Then the art of money-making frees a man from poverty; medicine from disease; and justice from intemperance and injustice?

POLUS: That is evident.

SOCRATES: Which, then, is the best of these three?

POLUS: Will you enumerate them?

SOCRATES: Money-making, medicine, and justice. → best art according to Polus

POLUS: Justice, Socrates, far excels the two others.

SOCRATES: And justice, if the best, gives the greatest pleasure or advantage or both?

POLUS: Yes.

SOCRATES: But is the being healed a pleasant thing, and are those who are being healed pleased?

POLUS: I think not.

185

SOCRATES: A useful thing, then?

POLUS: Yes.

SOCRATES: Yes, because the patient is delivered from a great evil; and this is the advantage of enduring the pain—that you get well?

POLUS: Certainly.

SOCRATES: And would he be the happier man in his bodily condition, who is healed, or who never was out of health?

POLUS: Clearly he who was never out of health.

SOCRATES: Yes; for happiness surely does not consist in being delivered from evils, but in never having had them.

POLUS: True.

SOCRATES: And suppose the case of two persons who have some evil in their bodies, and that one of them is healed and delivered from evil, and another is not healed, but retains the evil—which of them is the most miserable?

POLUS: Clearly he who is not healed.

SOCRATES: And was not punishment said by us to be a deliverance from the greatest of evils, which is vice?

POLUS: True.

SOCRATES: And justice punishes us, and makes us more just, and is the medicine of our vice?

POLUS: True.

SOCRATES: He, then, has the first place in the scale of happiness who has never had vice in his soul; for this has been shown to be the greatest of evils.

POLUS: Clearly.

SOCRATES: And he has the second place, who is delivered from vice?

POLUS: True.

SOCRATES: That is to say, he who receives admonition and rebuke and punishment?

POLUS: Yes.

SOCRATES: Then he lives worst, who, having been unjust, has no deliverance from injustice?

POLUS: Certainly.

SOCRATES: That is, he lives worst who commits the greatest crimes, and who, being the most unjust of men, succeeds in escaping rebuke or correction or punishment; and this, as you say, has been accomplished by Archelaus and other tyrants and rhetoricians and potentates?[9]

POLUS: True.

SOCRATES: May not their way of proceeding, my friend, be compared to the conduct of a person who is afflicted with the worst of diseases and yet contrives not to pay the penalty to the physician for his sins against his constitution, and will not be cured, because, like a child, he is afraid of the pain of being burned or cut:—Is not that a parallel case?

---

[9] Interesting and fruitful comparison with the Republic.

POLUS: Yes, truly.

SOCRATES: He would seem as if he did not know the nature of health and bodily vigor; and if we are right, Polus, in our previous conclusions, they are in a like case who strive to evade justice, which they see to be painful, but are blind to the advantage which ensues from it, not knowing how far more miserable a companion a diseased soul is than a diseased body; a soul, I say, which is corrupt and unrighteous and unholy. And hence they do all that they can to avoid punishment and to avoid being released from the greatest of evils; they provide themselves with money and friends, and cultivate to the utmost their powers of persuasion. But if we, Polus, are right, do you see what follows, or shall we draw out the consequences in form?

POLUS: If you please.

SOCRATES: Is it not a fact that injustice, and the doing of injustice, is the greatest of evils?

POLUS: That is quite clear.

SOCRATES: And further, that to suffer punishment is the way to be released from this evil?

POLUS: True.

SOCRATES: And not to suffer, is to perpetuate the evil?

POLUS: Yes.

SOCRATES: To do wrong, then, is second only in the scale of evils; but to do wrong and not to be punished, is first and greatest of all?

POLUS: That is true.

SOCRATES: Well, and was not this the point in dispute, my friend? You deemed Archelaus happy, because he was a very great criminal and unpunished: I, on the other hand, maintained that he or any other who like him has done wrong and has not been punished, is, and ought to be, the most miserable of all men; and that the doer of injustice is more miserable than the sufferer; and he who escapes punishment, more miserable than he who suffers.—Was not that what I said?

POLUS: Yes.

SOCRATES: And it has been proved to be true?

POLUS: Certainly.

SOCRATES: Well, Polus, but if this is true, where is the great use of rhetoric? If we admit what has been just now said, every man ought in every way to guard himself against doing wrong, for he will thereby suffer great evil?

POLUS: True.

SOCRATES: And if he, or any one about whom he cares, does wrong, he ought of his own accord to go where he will be immediately punished; he will run to the judge, as he would to the physician, in order that the disease of injustice may not be rendered chronic and become the incurable cancer of the soul; must we not allow this consequence, Polus, if our former admissions are to stand:—is any other inference consistent with them?

POLUS: To that, Socrates, there can be but one answer.

SOCRATES: Then rhetoric is of no use to us, Polus, in helping a man to excuse his own injustice, that of his parents or friends, or children or country; but may be of use to any one who holds that instead of excusing he ought to accuse—himself above all, and in the next degree his family or any of his friends who may be doing wrong; he should bring to light the iniquity and not conceal it, that so the wrong-doer may suffer and be made whole; and he should even force himself and others not to shrink, but with closed eyes like brave men to let the physician operate with knife or searing iron, not regarding the pain, in the hope of attaining the good and the honorable; let him who has done things worthy of stripes, allow himself to be scourged, if of bonds, to be bound, if of a fine, to be fined, if of exile, to be exiled, if of death, to die, himself being the first to accuse himself and his own relations, and using rhetoric to this end, that his and their unjust actions may be made manifest, and that they themselves may be delivered from injustice, which is the greatest evil. Then, Polus, rhetoric would indeed be useful. Do you say 'Yes' or 'No' to that?

POLUS: To me, Socrates, what you are saying appears very strange, though probably in agreement with your premises.

SOCRATES: Is not this the conclusion, if the premises are not disproven?

POLUS: Yes; it certainly is.

SOCRATES: And from the opposite point of view, if indeed it be our duty to harm another, whether an enemy or not--I except the case of self-defense--then I have to be upon my guard--but if my enemy injures a third person, then in every sort of way, by word as well as deed, I should try to prevent his being punished, or appearing before the judge; and if he appears, I should contrive that he should escape, and not suffer punishment: if he has stolen a sum of money, let him keep what he has stolen and spend it on him and his, regardless of religion and justice; and if he have done things worthy of death, let him not die, but rather be immortal in his wickedness; or, if this is not possible, let him at any rate be allowed to live as long as he can. For such purposes, Polus, rhetoric may be useful, but is of small if of any use to him who is not intending to commit injustice; at least, there was no such use discovered by us in the previous discussion.

Made in the USA
Las Vegas, NV
16 August 2023

76178080R00105